SIGHTSINGING COMPLETE

Sixth Edition

Bruce Benward
University of Wisconsin, Madison

Maureen A. Carr
Pennsylvania State University, University Park

McGraw-Hill College

Boston   Burr Ridge, IL   Dubuque, IA   Madison, WI   New York   San Francisco   St. Louis
Bangkok   Bogotá   Caracas   Lisbon   London   Madrid
Mexico City   Milan   New Delhi   Seoul   Singapore   Sydney   Taipei   Toronto

McGraw-Hill College

A Division of The McGraw·Hill Companies

SIGHTSINGING COMPLETE, SIXTH EDITION

 This book is printed on recycled, acid-free paper containing 10% postconsumer waste.

1 2 3 4 5 6 7 8 9 0 QPD/QPD 9 3 2 1 0 9 8

ISBN 0–697–34395–2

Editorial director: *Phil Butcher*
Sponsoring editor: *Christopher Freitag*
Developmental editor: *JoElaine Retzler*
Marketing manager: *David S. Patterson*
Project manager: *Susan J. Brusch*
Senior production supervisor: *Sandra Hahn*
Freelance design coordinator: *Mary L. Christianson*
Photo research coordinator: *John C. Leland*
Compositor: *A-R Editions, Inc.*
Typeface: *10/12 Times Roman*
Printer: *Quebecor Printing Book Group/Dubuque, IA*

Freelance cover designer: *Sheilah Barrett*
Cover image: © *UniPhoto*

www.mhhe.com

In Memoriam

Bernard M. Carr
(1907–1989)

Emily J. Carr
(1907–1993)

Contents

Unit 4

Unit 5

Unit 6

Unit 7

Unit 8

Unit 9

Unit 10

Unit 11

Unit 12

Unit 13

Unit 14

Unit 15

Unit 16

Preface

To the Student

The Goal of Sightsinging: Coming "On Line" with Musical Notation

Because music is the most abstract of all the arts, it is necessary for composers to translate their musical ideas into notation. With modern-day technology, composers can play directly into a synthesizer and have a computer instantly notate their musical ideas. Ultimately, though, whether notating the old-fashioned way by hand or by using computers, composers must rely on the symbols of musical notation if they are to develop a "readership" for their works.

If we are to become part of a thoughtful readership, we must develop the aural skills that will enable us to reverse the compositional process of sound into symbol to one of symbol into sound. Just as painters speak of the "thinking eye" (Klee), playwrights and poets of the "mind's eye" (Shakespeare), and psychologists of the "soul's eye," musicians are trained to develop a "hearing eye." For only when we are able to translate musical symbols from the concrete level of musical notation into sounds will we be able to approximate the abstract musical ideas that the composer was trying to communicate in the first place.

The purpose of *Sightsinging Complete* is to enable students to develop a "hearing eye" in order to come "on line" with musical notation. In this way they can participate more fully in the thoughtful readership that composers deserve. The task of observing a musical score with thoughtful and hearing eyes is the most significant outcome of the four-semester sequence of courses for which this textbook is designed.

The idea of replaying a work of art in one's mind is not unique to music. For example, a scholar of Elizabethan drama encourages the reader of a play by Shakespeare "to rehearse the play in his [or her] mind, considering the text in detail as an actor would, **hearing** and **seeing** each moment."[1] The student of music has precisely the same goal: to be able to rehearse the musical

score in his or her mind, considering the musical notation in detail as a conductor, performer, or composer would—**hearing** and **seeing** each moment.

Helpful Strategies

Sightsinging is one of the most practical means that students have of demonstrating to their instructors the progress they are making in "hearing" the notation they are "seeing." For this reason, various strategies exist to help students improve their aural skills.

1. **Syllables or numbers.** Learn thoroughly whatever syllable or numbering system your instructor recommends. To take the guesswork out of sightsinging, it is important to "know" the scale degree of all melody notes and to communicate that information to your instructor—as well as to yourself.

2. **Intervals.** Knowing what E sounds like when you are presently singing C is something to get accustomed to. At first it may be difficult, but when you learn that from C to E is the same distance as from F to A or G to B, your problem is diminished considerably. Learning to sing intervals (distance between pitches) is an absolute must.

3. **Familiarity with the scale.** Figure out the key of each melody and sing the scale before attacking the melody itself.

4. **Reference tones.** Isolate the 1st, 3rd, and 5th scale degrees and sing them until memorized. Then, for a while at least, circle all 1st, 3rd, and 5th scale degrees in the melody. These are called reference tones.

5. **The tonic note.** You should be able to pause anywhere in a melody and sing the tonic (1st scale degree) pitch immediately. Try it a few times just to make sure you can do it.

6. **"Hearing" what you are "seeing."** Practice scanning melodies—thinking (rather than singing) what each pitch sounds like. The sooner you can do this, the closer you will be to developing a "hearing eye."

7. **Steady tempo.** Avoid starts and stops in sightsinging. Doing so means that the tempo you selected may be too fast—your voice gets ahead of your mind.

[1] Robert Hapgood, "Shakespeare and the Included Spectator" (commentary on John Russell Brown, "Laughter in the Last Plays," *Shakespeare's Plays in Performance* [London, 1967] In *Reinterpretations of Elizabethan Drama*, edited by Norman Rabkin, p. 133. New York: Columbia University Press, 1969) (emphasis added). The essay was also cited in Michael Cohen, *Hamlet in My Mind's Eye.* Athens and London: University of Georgia Press, 1989.

8. **Rhythm.** Trying to figure out the next pitch and rhythm at the same time may be overwhelming at first. Before singing, tap out the rhythm of the entire melody. This "divide and conquer" technique will help considerably, and you will soon be able to coordinate both.

To the Instructor

Special to this Sixth Edition

This new edition contains the following revisions:

1. **A reordering of the sections within each unit.** Each unit opens with a section devoted to rhythm. (In the previous edition, each unit ended with rhythm, except in the combined sightsinging and ear-training book, in which each unit began with rhythm.) For the sake of clarity, the notation of rhythm modules and phrases is placed on a single line rather than on a staff of five lines.

    The second section of each unit contains models and melodic fragments for interval study. In the previous edition these topics appeared in separate sections within each unit.

2. **A thread of creativity.** Students are guided through a process to help them create coherent phrases at the ends of sections A and B throughout the first fifteen units.

3. **New materials located at the Schomburg Center for Research in Black Culture (a division of the New York Public Library) and the Arts Library of the Pennsylvania State University.** Through the resources of the Schomburg Center and Pattee Library, additional materials having to do with the music of Jamaica, Trinidad, Haiti, and Santeria were located. Other additions include Creole folk songs, French Canadian folk-singing games, Jewish folk songs, songs from the northern woods, Ethiopian chants, Irish ballads, songs by Clara Schumann, Chris Smith (who wrote "Ballin' the Jack"), and other twentieth-century composers including Igor Stravinsky, Kurt Weill, Benjamin Britten, William Bolcom and Ellen Taaffe Zwilich.

4. **An index of tunes.** This edition provides an index of melodies listed in alphabetical order by composers.

5. **A home page on the World Wide Web for those users who want to establish a dialogue with the authors about teaching techniques.** This is also an opportunity to provide sample syllabi for instructors who have questions about the pacing of materials.

Format of the Text

The text is divided into sixteen units, and, except for the last two (twentieth century) units, in which sections C and D are merged, each contains five sections: A, B, C, D, and E. Each section constitutes a **track,** or procedure, that is developed throughout the sixteen units.

Section A: Rhythm

Each rhythm unit begins with rhythm modules in small units that are then combined into phrases. Students are asked to create coherent phrases from the modules that they have just learned.

Rhythms syllables are provided throughout the text for those instructors who wish to use them. Because rhythmic complications can be sought out and drilled more knowledgeably with a system, the authors encourage the use of some kind of nomenclature, whether it be the one printed in this text or another one favored by the instructor.

Section B: Models and Melodic Fragments for Interval Singing

This section aims to provide students with melodic patterns derived from music literature. Initially, the focus is on **hearing** and **singing** before **reading,** so that students will become familiar with melodic patterns aurally before they are asked to read them in notation. The process of melodic **fragmentation** serves a number of purposes. The brevity of each fragment (at least in the earlier units) allows the students to focus on the specific musical element or elements of the given harmonies. Of necessity, the melodic fragments in the later units become longer than those of the earlier ones because the "vocabulary" is more complicated in chromatic and atonal structures.

At the end of each section, students are asked to create coherent melodies on the basis of the melodic fragments they have just learned.

(To give students the experience of reading through all the key signatures represented in the circle of 5ths, an attempt is made to systematically introduce new key signatures.)

Section C: Shorter and Easier Melodies to Be Sung at Performance Tempo

This section provides an opportunity for students to test their sightsinging skills for continuity, accuracy, and musicality. These melodies are shorter, contain few problem intervals or rhythms, require little or no preparation, and are intended to be sung at sight on the first attempt.

Section D: Melodies for More Comprehensive Study

Section D of units 1–14 are made up entirely of tonal melodies, lending themselves quite appropriately to solfeggio, or number systems. Because the materials in Units 15 and 16 are more contemporary, systems such as "neutral syllable," chromatic fixed-Do, or integers 0–11 are more appropriate.

Section E: Ensemble Excerpts

Ensemble singing is often overlooked. Students must learn to create a balanced ensemble sound and at the same time not be distracted or allow concentration to be interrupted.

The Available Systems

Most instructors who have taught sightsinging for years have either chosen or developed a system with which they feel comfortable. Those who are teaching the course for the first time may be interested in the variety of approaches:

Moveable Do

1. In the moveable Do system, the tonic pitch is Do in all major keys, whether it be C, A♭, or F♯.

2. In one moveable Do system, the tonic pitch of minor keys is represented by La. In the other system, the tonic pitch of minor is represented by Do.

Fixed Do

1. Do is always the same note (usually C) regardless of the key.

2. Protagonists of fixed Do point out that because particular lines or spaces of each staff are always associated with the same syllable, the system encourages true reading skills and is thus superior to any other method. Others believe that fixed Do, compared to moveable Do, is more difficult to master and does not accentuate as clearly the basic pattern of whole and half steps in major and minor scales.

Moveable Numbers

1. Similar in design to moveable Do, numbers (most often 1–7) are substituted for the solfeggio syllables. The tonic note becomes "1."

2. Some instructors prefer numbers because they believe numbers are more familiar to students and are easier to teach, but others find numbers less euphonious and laden with confusing implications.

Fixed Numbers

A system similar to fixed Do, "0" is always the same pitch class (usually C).

Seven-Syllable or Number Systems

Systems made up of seven symbols may be applied to moveable Do, fixed Do, moveable numbers, or fixed numbers. Because only diatonic pitches are accounted for, students are expected to "think" accidentals when they occur. Typical examples are as follows:

Some Moveable and Fixed Systems in Major Keys

G-Major Scale	G	A	B	C	D	E	F♯	G
Seven-syllable moveable Do:	Do	Re	Mi	Fa	Sol	La	Ti	Do
Seven-syllable fixed Do:	Sol	La	Ti	Do	Re	Mi	Fa	Sol
Seven-number moveable system:	1	2	3	4	5	6	7	1
Seven-number fixed system:	5	6	7	1	2	3	4	5

Some Moveable Systems for Minor Keys

G-Harmonic Minor Scale	G	A	B♭	C	D	E♭	F♯	G
La-based minor:	La	Ti	Do	Re	Mi	Fa	Si	La
Do-based minor:	Do	Re	Me	Fa	Sol	Le	Ti	Do
Six-based minor:	6	7	1	2	3	4	5	6
One-based minor:	1	2	3	4	5	6	7	1

Twelve-Syllable or Number Systems

The use of twelve symbols makes possible a label for all pitch classes of the octave. Some examples are:

G-Major Scale:	G	(G♯)	A	(A♯)	B	C	(C♯)	D	(D♯)	E	(E♯)	F♯
Twelve-tone moveable Do:	#Do	Di	Re	Ri	Mi	Fa	Fi	Sol	Si	La	Li	Ti
Twelve-tone fixed Do:	†Sol	Si	La	Li	Ti	Do	Di	Re	Ri	Mi	Mis	Fi
Twelve-tone fixed numbers:	*7	8	9	10	11	0	1	2	3	4	5	6

#Descending order is: Do Ti Te La Le Sol Se Fa Mi Me Re Ra Do
†Descending order is: Sol Se Fa Mi Me Re Ra Do Ti Te La Le Sol
*Some instructors prefer the numbers 1–12 rather than 0–11.

Acknowledgments

Thanks go to the following people who reviewed this text in various editions and stages of development: Mary A. Burroughs, East Carolina University; Robert Clifford, University of Arizona; Gary Karpinski, University of Oregon; Sandra Matthes, Liberty University; Donald Para, California State University, Long Beach; David N. Patterson, University of Massachusetts, Boston; Tressa Reisetter; Rodney Rogers, Arizona State University; Robert A. Stephenson, Northern Michigan University; Nancy E. Whitman, Kearney State College.

Unit 1

A Rhythm—Simple Meter: One-, Two-, and Three-Beat Values

Section 1. Modules in Simple Meter

Using a neutral syllable, sing the patterns in each of the given modules. Begin by repeating each module several times. Then treat the successive modules as a continuous exercise.

Notice that the values of the notes and rests in these modules encompass one, two, or three beats. The **quarter note** represents the beat in meters such as [$\frac{2}{4}$], [$\frac{3}{4}$], and [$\frac{4}{4}$]; the **eighth note** in [$\frac{3}{8}$] and [$\frac{4}{8}$]; the **sixteenth note** in [$\frac{4}{16}$]; the **half note** in [$\frac{4}{2}$]; and so on. In subsequent chapters you will learn how to divide beats. This process will help you understand the difference between simple and compound meter.

For a complete explanation of the differences between simple meter and compound meter, see Benward and White, *Music in Theory and Practice,* vol. 1 (6th ed.), p. 17.

Use the conducting patterns shown below, if your instructor recommends you do so.

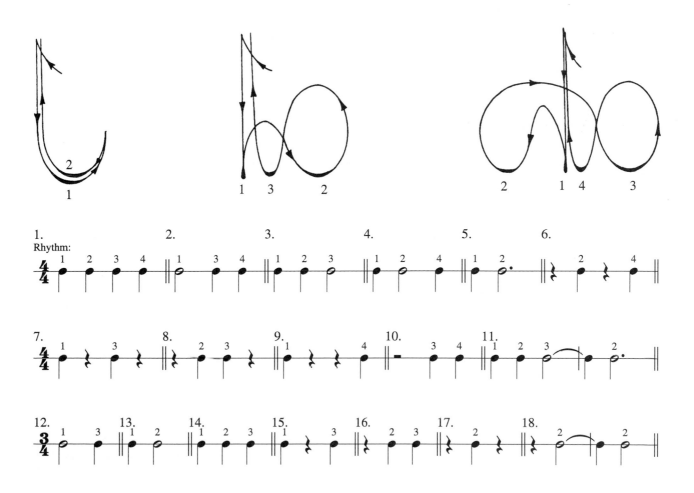

Section 2. Phrases in Simple Meter

Eventually, you will learn to internalize the beat, but in the early stages of learning to read rhythms you can use a number of different procedures:

1. Clap the meter and sing the rhythm (use a neutral syllable or the system of rhythm syllables recommended by your instructor).
2. Sing the meter and clap the rhythm.
3. Tap the meter with one hand and the rhythm with the other.
4. Half the class taps the meter while the other half claps the rhythm.

1.

Section 3. Creating a Coherent Phrase in Simple Meter

Return to section 1 and select three or four rhythm modules. Place them in an order that would create a coherent four-measure phrase. Here is an example based on modules 11, 4, and 3:

Write your solution on the following line:

Use a neutral syllable to sing your phrase and have your classmates identify which modules you selected and the order in which you sang them. At some future date, return to this phrase and add the melodic dimension.

B Diatonic Models and Melodic Fragments for Interval Singing: M2nd and m2nd.

Section 1. Diatonic Models

(a) Vocalise descending from $\hat{5}$ to $\hat{1}$

Neighboring tone figures in combination with passing tone figures outlining a descending line from scale degrees 5 to 1. Exercises 1–3 combine neighboring and passing tone figures to fill in a descending line from scale degrees 5 to 1 in major and minor. These passages (or *vocalises*) may be used as a way to establish the key for tonal exercises and melodies throughout the book.

Procedure

Exercises 1–3

Step 1. Your instructor sings or plays figure 1 (major) as a means of establishing the key.

Step 2. Repeat (sing) the same figure your instructor provides in step 1.

Step 3. For additional practice, follow the same procedure in each major key by moving down a perfect 5th (or up a perfect 4th), first to F major, then to B♭, E♭, and so on. See the following model:

(b) Vocalise descending from $\hat{1}$ to $\hat{5}$ and ascending from $\hat{5}$ to $\hat{1}$

Double neighboring tone figures at cadential points will help you confirm the tonic of a key. This model will be useful to you in writing creative exercises. As with the previous vocalise, this passage may be used as a way to establish the key for tonal exercises and melodies throughout the book.

Procedure

Exercise 4

Follow the same procedure for singing this vocalise in different keys down a 5th (or up a 4th).

FM: B♭M: E♭M:

4. C Major

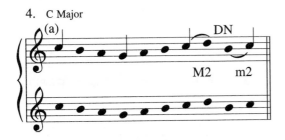

(a)   DN

M2   m2

Section 2. Melodic Fragments in F Major

These melodic fragments are taken from music literature for the purpose of providing a musical context for the intervals M2nd and m2nd. Examples of neighboring, passing, and double neighboring tones occur in abundance.

Procedure

1. Your instructor establishes the key for each of the fragments, using one of the *vocalises* taught in exercises 1, 2, 3, or 4 transposed to the appropriate pitch level.
2. Sing the following excerpts and identify neighboring, passing, and double neighboring tone figures as well as intervals.

1. Lord Have Mercy—Requiem Mass. Gregorian Chant

♩ = 144

2. Come Holy Spirit—Pentecost (abridged). Gregorian Chant

♩ = 144

3. Praise—Passover. Adapted from Songs of the Babylonian Jews

♩ = 144

4. Forgiveness (a specific series of blessings). Adapted from Songs of the Babylonian Jews

♩ = 144

5. The Coulin (lament). Adapted from a Gaelic lament.

Section 3. Creating a Coherent Chant

Return to section 2 and select two or three segments of melodic fragments 1–5. Place them in an order that would create a coherent chant. Here is an example based on the first and last segments of fragment 4 and the first segment of fragment 5.

C   Melodies (Major): M2 and m2

1. Establish the key for each of the following melodies by singing one of the *vocalises* presented earlier.
2. Using syllables or numbers, sing the melody.
3. Try to differentiate between neighboring and passing tone figures as you read each melody.

1. Scale: C Major

2. Scale: G Major

3. Scale: F Major

4. Scale: D Major

5. Scale: B-flat Major

6. Scale: A Major

7. Scale: E-flat Major

8. Scale: E Major

9. Scale: A-flat Major

10. Scale: B Major

11. Scale: C Major
Moderato

12. Scale: G Major
Allegro

13. Scale: F Major

14. Scale: B-flat Major

15. Scale: D Major

The last four measures of number 16 are in contrary motion to the first four.

16. Scale: E-flat Major

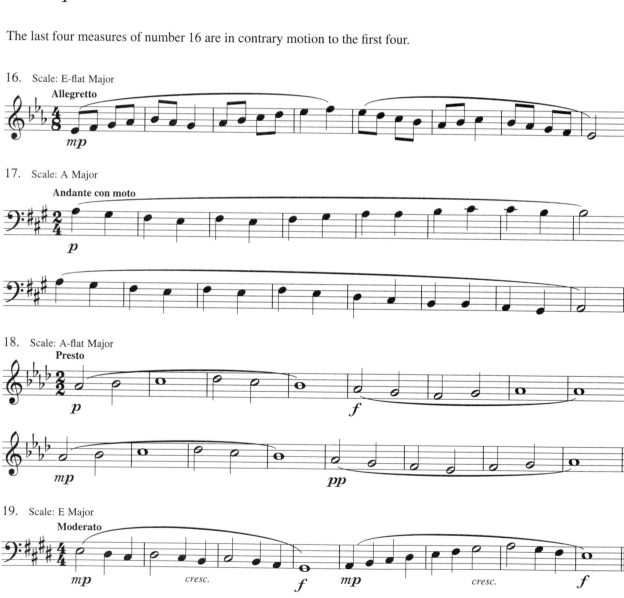

17. Scale: A Major

18. Scale: A-flat Major

19. Scale: E Major

20. Scale: C Major

D   Melodies (Major): P5, P4, M3, and m3 within the Tonic Triad and M2 and m2

1. Establish the key for each of the following melodies by singing a *vocalise*.
2. Using syllables or numbers, sing the melody.
3. Try to consider the elements of the triad as *reference tones*.

E   Ensemble—Two Voices: M2 and m2

This two-voice section is intended to provide practice in **ensemble** singing. The melody lines are similar to those found in part C of this unit, but now you must learn to think in two melodic dimensions. For individual practice, you could sing one line and play the other line at the keyboard. This would be excellent preparation for the classroom experience of singing in ensemble.

Follow the procedures outlined in part C for establishing the key.

Unit 2

A   Rhythm—Compound Meter: Triple Division of the Beat

Section 1. Modules in Compound Meter

Using a neutral syllable, sing each of the given modules. Begin by repeating each module several times. Then treat the successive modules as a continuous exercise.

Notice that each beat in these modules is divisible by three. This triple division of the beat allows us to determine whether these modules are in compound meter as opposed to simple meter. **Each beat in the compound meter of [$\frac{6}{8}$] is a dotted quarter note.** Therefore, in [$\frac{6}{8}$] there are two beats, each divisible by three; in [$\frac{9}{8}$] three beats, each divisible by three; and so on.

For a complete explanation of the division of the beat in compound meter, see Benward and White, *Music in Theory and Practice,* vol. 1 (6th ed.), pp. 17–18. An explanation of duple division of the beat in simple meter is given in unit 3.

Rhythm Syllables

Select one of the two following systems if your instructor recommends you do so.

Pronunciation:
AN as in *ANOTHER*
DU as in *DUMP*
LA as in *LARVA*
LE as in *LEE*

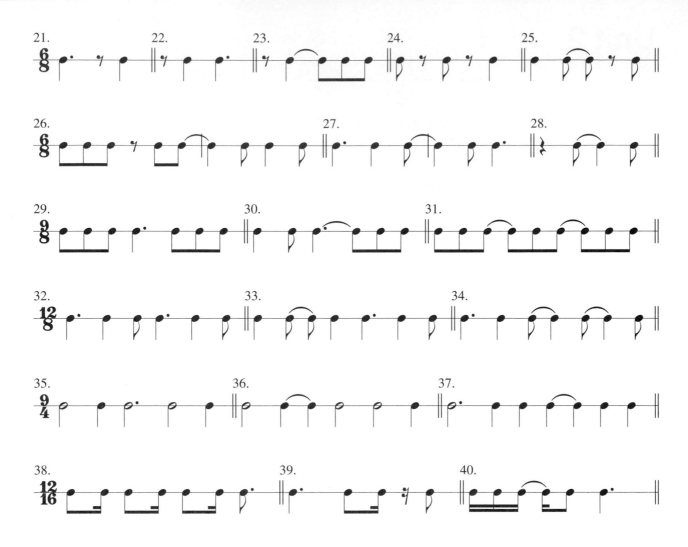

Section 2. Phrases in Compound Meter

For numbers 1–5, follow the procedures outlined in unit 1A, section 2. For the two-part exercises (6–9), the instructor should assign students to each part. Students should also be encouraged to practice these two-part exercises individually, using the left hand for tapping out the lower part and the right hand the upper part.

3.

4.

5.

6. Rhythmic ostinato plus rhythmic imitation

7. Rhythmic alternation (examples also of rhythmic hocket)

8. Rhythmic imitation

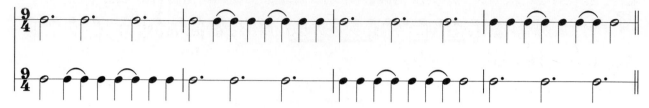

9. Rhythmic imitation

Section 3. Creating a Coherent Phrase in Compound Meter

Return to section 1 and select four modules in the same meter. Place them in an order that would create a coherent four-measure phrase. Here is an example:

25.   24.   21.   22.

Write your solution on the following stave (or staves in case you decide to write a two-voice composition):

Using a neutral syllable, sing your phrase and have your classmates identify which modules you selected and the order in which you sang them. At some future date, return to this phrase and add the melodic dimension. (If you have written a two-voice composition, perform one part on the piano while singing the other part with a neutral syllable.)

B Diatonic Models and Melodic Fragments for Interval Singing: P5, P4, M3, m3, M2, and m2

Section 1. Diatonic Models

These models anticipate the melodic fragments in the next section.

(a) Intervals of the 3rd Outlining P5s in Major Keys

Use a G major vocalise as a warm-up. Sing this exercise as written (in G major), and then transpose the entire set down a P5 to the key of C major. Continue the process through the keys of F, B♭, E♭, and so on.

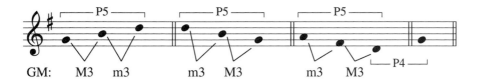

(b) Passing Tone Figures in Minor Filling in 3rds

Follow the same procedure for passing tone figures in major keys. Use a vocalise in E minor (relative minor). For exercises in parallel minor, use a vocalise in G minor.

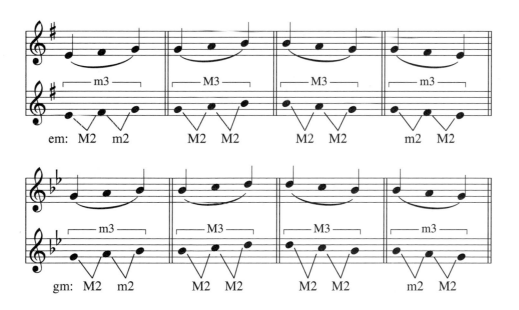

(c) Intervals of the P4, P5, and M3 Supporting a Melodic Ascent from $\hat{1}$–$\hat{3}$

Use a G major vocalise as a warm-up. After singing the intervals that outline scale degrees 1–3, sing the entire pattern in different keys as shown in the model:

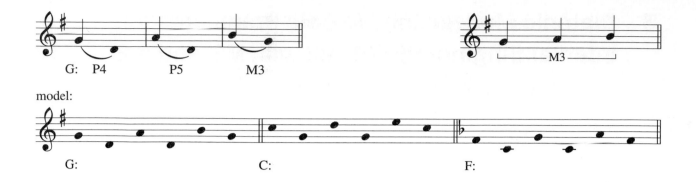

model:

G: C: F:

Section 2. Melodic Fragments in G Major (E Minor and G Minor)

These melodic fragments are taken from music literature for the purpose of providing a musical context for the intervals introduced in the previous section.

Follow the procedure outlined in unit 1B, section 2.

1.   Mozart   German Dance no. 5, K. 509 (transposed)

Bach   Chorale 48, *Ach wie nichtig, ach wie flüchtig* (Ah, How Empty! Ah, How Fleeting!) (transposed)
2a.

Bach   Chorale 48, *Ach wie nichtig, ach wie flüchtig* (Ah, How Empty! Ah, How Fleeting!) (transposed)
2b.

3.   Mozart   *Sanctus* from *Requiem*, K. 626, (transposed)

Section 3. Creating a Coherent Melody

Return to section 2 and select two or three segments of melodic fragments that would create a coherent melody. It may be necessary to change the meter and rhythm of certain segments, depending on your choices. Here is an example based on measures 1 and 2 of fragment 1 and measures 2 and 3 of fragment 4.

C Melodies: P5, P4, M3, and m3 within the Tonic Triad and M2, and m2

The melodic content of this section focuses on some leaps within the tonic triad (M3, m3, P5, P4) as well as step-wise motion (M2 and m2) in C major.

These drills, although valuable for review and practice in singing at performance tempo, are suitable also for developing the art of clef reading as a means of transposing from one key to another. For example, the same phrase is used in both number 1 and number 11, except that in number 11 the alto clef is introduced. This places middle C (c') on the middle line. The alto clef in number 11 makes it possible to transpose number 1 to the key of D major without changing the position of any of the notes on the staff.

Procedure

1. In your mind, replace the **treble** clef in number 2 with an **alto** clef (see number 11 to visualize an alto clef).
2. Because all melodies in this section are in C major, you know that number 2 begins on the dominant (5, or Sol).
3. When you visualize number 2 with an alto clef, the first pitch is A (below middle C). A is now the dominant (5, or Sol) and D is the tonic of the melody.
4. Imagine two sharps (F♯ and C♯) in the signature and sing the melody the same way as you sing it in C major with a treble clef.
5. If you sing the melody in the alto clef, it will be a 7th lower than in treble, but most melodies in this book are intended to be sung in whatever range the singer finds most comfortable.
6. If you have trouble reading in the alto clef, check your accuracy by going back to C major with a treble clef and singing the melody again.
7. Your unfamiliarity with this new clef will disappear presently, and you will have learned a valuable new skill that you may use many times later on.

D Melodies (Major): P5, P4, M3, and m3 within the Tonic Triad and M2 and m2

Section 1. Excerpts from Beethoven and Haydn

The following melodies excerpted from music literature illustrate the same intervals presented in part C of this unit.

Numbers 1–10 are from Beethoven's symphonic works, and 11–20 are from Haydn's keyboard compositions. For the purposes of this unit, some melodies have been slightly altered or abridged. The authors of this book adjusted the melodies to ensure a comfortable singing range and to stay within the rhythmic and melodic limitations imposed by the materials of the first two units. However, for those excerpts from Beethoven symphonies that were adapted, the original version is provided as well.

Sing these melodies using whatever procedures your instructor requests.

1. Adapted from Beethoven   Symphony no. 6, op. 68, III

2. Adapted from Beethoven   Symphony no. 6, op. 68, III

3. Beethoven   Symphony no. 6, op. 68, III

4. Adapted from Beethoven   Symphony no. 2, op. 36, III (Trio)

5. **Allegretto**

dolce
p

Adapted from Beethoven   Symphony no. 7, op. 92, III

6. **Presto**

dolce
p

original

Adapted from Beethoven   Symphony no. 7, op. 92, IV

7. **Allegro con brio**

ff

original

ff   *staccato*

Adapted from Beethoven   Symphony no. 5, op. 67, IV

8. **Allegro**

ff

original

Adapted from Beethoven   Symphony no. 8, op. 93, I

9. **Allegro vivace e con brio**

f

p *dolce*

original

19.

Adapted from Haydn   Minuet in G Major, Hob. XVI:11, III

20.   Allegro assai

Adapted from Haydn   Nine Early Sonatas, 9, III

Section 2. Amish Songs and Hymn Tunes

The following are adapted Amish songs and hymn tunes.

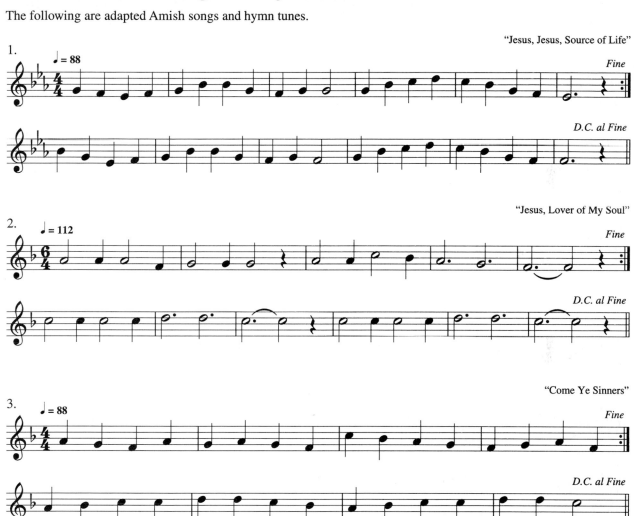

"Jesus, Jesus, Source of Life"

1.   ♩ = 88

"Jesus, Lover of My Soul"

2.   ♩ = 112

"Come Ye Sinners"

3.   ♩ = 88

"The Great Physician"

4.

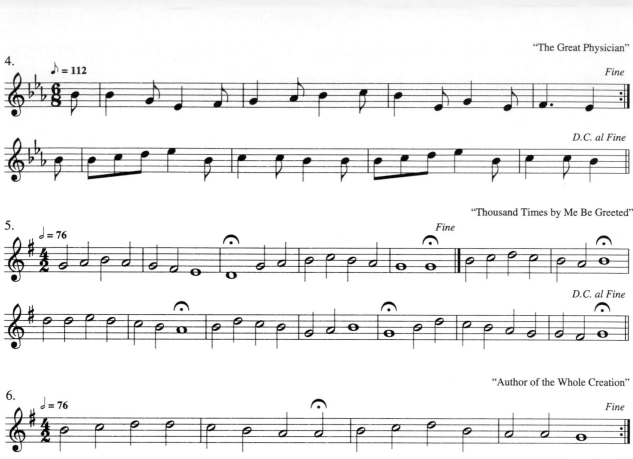

"Thousand Times by Me Be Greeted"

5.

"Author of the Whole Creation"

6.

"When the Due Time Had Taken Place"

7.

"Praise God Forever"

8.

E   Ensembles—Two Voices: P5, P4, M3, and m3 within the Tonic Triad and M2 and m2

The first three ensemble excerpts are from Beethoven's *Missa Solemnis,* op. 123: (1) Gloria, (2) Credo, and (3) Benedictus. Each melodic line operates within the same intervallic restrictions of this unit. The fourth excerpt, by Orlande de Lassus, provides another setting of the Benedictus written much earlier than the Beethoven.

Because each excerpt is imitative, sing each line as a separate melodic exercise before you try to put the two together. The texts from Gloria, Credo, and Benedictus are provided, although you need not use words in performing these.

* See section A of this unit for compound meter.
  As a warm-up for ensemble singing, each line should be performed as a solo exercise.
  When the students are ready to sing in ensemble, the instructor should provide the first few notes of each part at entrances, either by singing with the students, or by articulating these patterns at the keyboard.

4.

Cantus

Be - ne - di - ctus, _____ qui ve -

Tenor

Be - ne - di - ctus, _____ qui

- nit   in no - mi - ne _____ Do -

ve - nit   in no - mi - ne Do -

- mi - ni, in no - mi - ne, _____   in no - mi - ne, _____

- mi - ni,   in no - mi - ne, _____   in no - mi - ne, _____

___ in no - mi - ne _____ Do - mi - ni.

___ in no - mi - ne _____ Do - mi - ni.

New York: Appleton-Century-Crofts, Inc.—G. Soderlund

Unit 3

A Rhythm—Simple Meter: Duple Division of the Beat

Section 1. Modules in Simple Meter

Using rhythm syllables or a neutral syllable, sing each of the given modules. Begin by repeating each module several times. Then treat the successive modules as a continuous exercise.

Notice that each beat in these modules is divisible by two. This duple division of the beat allows you to determine whether these modules are in simple meter or compound meter. **Each beat in the simple meter of [$\frac{4}{4}$] is a quarter note.** Therefore, in [$\frac{4}{4}$] there are four beats, each divisible by two; in [$\frac{3}{4}$] three beats, each divisible by two; and so on.

For a complete explanation of the division of the beat in simple meter, see Benward and White, *Music in Theory and Practice,* vol. 1 (6th ed.), p. 17.

Rhythm Syllables

Select one of the two following systems if your instructor recommends you do so.

Rhythm syllables:

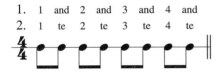

Examples:

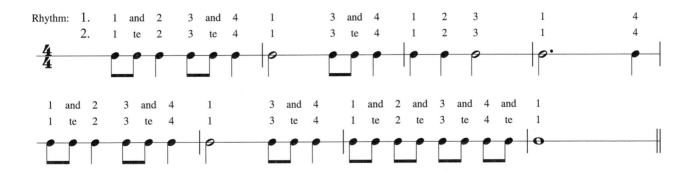

Calypso patterns related to song 5 in part D, section 2, of this unit.

Section 2. Phrases in Simple Meter with Duple Division of the Beat

For numbers 1–8, follow the procedures outlined in unit 1A, section 2. For the two-part exercises (9–10), follow the procedures outlined in unit 2A, section 2.

9. Rhythmic canon

10. Some rhythmic imitation

Section 3. Creating a Coherent Phrase in Simple Meter

Return to section 1 and select four modules in the same meter. Place them in an order that would create a coherent four-measure phrase. Here is an example:

Write your solution on the following line (or lines in case you decided to write a two-voice composition):

Using a neutral syllable, sing your phrase and have your classmates identify which modules you selected and the order in which you sang them. At some future date, return to this phrase and add the melodic dimension. (If you have written a two-voice composition, perform one part on the piano while singing the other part with a neutral syllable.)

B Diatonic Models and Melodic Fragments for Interval Singing: P8, P5, P4, M3, m3, M2, and m2

Section 1. Diatonic Models

These models anticipate the melodic fragments in the next section.

(a) Intervals Outlining the Tonic Triad and Dominant 7th Chord in Major

Use a D major vocalise as a warm-up. For extra practice, sing these models in each of the major keys, moving down by fourths or up by fifths. See the following examples:

1.

2.

(b) Intervals Emphasizing the Tonic Triad in Minor, with Special Emphasis on the Perfect 4th

Use a B minor vocalise as a warm-up. For extra practice, sing these models in each of the minor keys, moving down by 5ths or up by 4ths. Follow the same procedure for the D minor excerpts. See the following examples:

Section 2. Melodic Fragments in D Major (B Minor and D Minor)

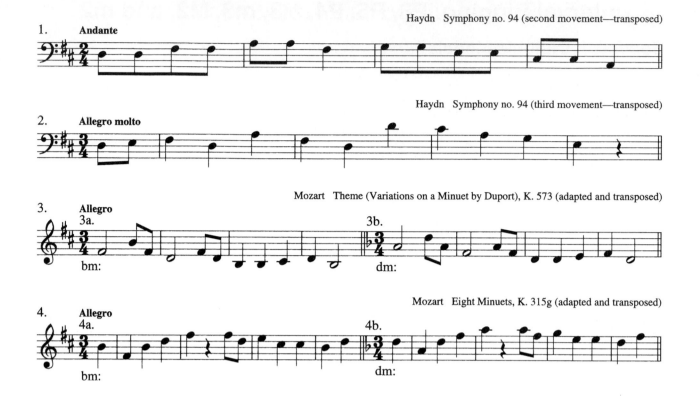

1. **Andante** — Haydn Symphony no. 94 (second movement—transposed)

2. **Allegro molto** — Haydn Symphony no. 94 (third movement—transposed)

3. **Allegro** — Mozart Theme (Variations on a Minuet by Duport), K. 573 (adapted and transposed)
   3a. bm: 3b. dm:

4. **Allegro** — Mozart Eight Minuets, K. 315g (adapted and transposed)
   4a. bm: 4b. dm:

Section 3. Creating a Coherent Melody

Return to section 2 and select two or three segments of melodic fragments that would create a coherent melody. It may be necessary to change the meter and rhythm of certain segments, depending on your choice. Here is an example based on measures 1 and 2 of fragment 3a and measures 3 and 4 of fragment 4a.

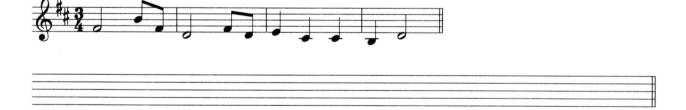

C Melodies (Major): P5, P4, M3, and m3 within the Tonic Triad and M2 and m2

Procedure for Completing Each Melody

1. Sing the scale upon which the melody is constructed. Use syllables or numbers as suggested by your instructor.
2. When you are familiar with the scale, sing each melody using the same syllables or numbers.
3. Circle the 1st, 3rd, and 5th scale degrees as *reference tones* if you encounter difficulty.
4. Remember that you learn *only* when you sing the correct pitch and syllable or number. So, do not hesitate to repeat a melody until you are satisfied that you have sung it correctly.
5. Tempo is important. Sing each melody slowly at first. If you can increase the tempo without making mistakes, do so.

From Games and Songs of American Children, composed and compiled by William Wells Newell. Copyright, 1883, 1903, by Harper and Brothers, Copyright, 1911, by Robert B. Stone CURWEN & Sons London, Copyright 1914 by Grace Cleveland Porter

From Games and Songs of American Children, composed and compiled by William Wells Newell. Copyright, 1883, 1903, by Harper and Brothers, Copyright, 1911, by Robert B. Stone CURWEN & Sons London, Copyright 1914 by Grace Cleveland Porter

D Melodies (Minor)

Section 1. P5, P4, M3, and m3 within the Tonic Triad

1. Sing the scale related to each exercise—as usual, with syllables or numbers.
2. Sing each melody with the same syllables or numbers.
3. For the moment, do not worry about the intervals formed by scale steps 1, 3, and 5. Think of these primarily as *reference tones*—tones from which other scale degrees may be located.

Section 2. Natural, Harmonic, and Melodic Minor

The first example shows a single melody repeated to illustrate the three forms of the minor scale. Sing all three forms, one after the other, and note the effect created by each. Examples 2–4 are in natural minor. Example 5 combines features of natural minor and harmonic minor. For a complete explanation of natural, harmonic, and melodic minor, see Benward and White, *Music in Theory and Practice,* vol. 1 (6th ed.), pp. 33–35.

"Land of the Humming Bird" (abridged) Words and Music by Lionel Belasco and Leighla Whipper, from *Calypso Rhythm Songs.* Copyright 1944 by Mills Music, 1619 Broadway, N.Y.

Section 3. P5, P4, M3, and m3 within the Tonic Triad and M2 and m2

Follow procedures printed in part D, section 1, of this unit.

Section 4. Transposition and Inversion

The first three examples of Gregorian chant are modal in character and are transcribed in modern notation. If sung as printed, these melodies will afford a valuable opportunity to get acquainted with music written before the advent of the major/minor system.

For some additional practice in clef reading and transposition:

1. Transpose number 1 (*Kyrie XI—Orbis factor*). When you visualize the alto clef, think of the melody as being in E minor (Aeolian mode), so include F♯ in the signature.
2. Transpose number 2 (*Sanctus IX—Cum jubilo*). This was originally considered to be in the Ionian mode (now our major mode). When you visualize the alto clef, also add an F♯ to the key signature. The starting note is d'.
3. Melodies 3 and 4 are closely related. The *Kyrie IX* (Cum jubilo) (number 3) is the source for Josquin's *Missa de Beata Virgine* (number 4). The alto voice is shown here. When you visualize the alto clef, see whether you can figure out the correct signatures.
4. Melodies 5 and 6 are from Contrapunctus XII of Bach's *Art of the Fugue;* number 6 is the melodic inversion of number 5.

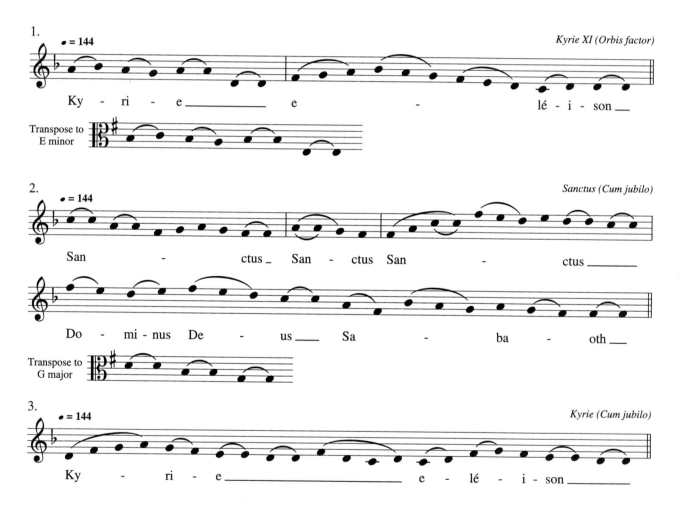

4.

Josquin des Prés *Kyrie eleison—Missa De Beate Virgine*

5.

Bach *Die Kunst der Fuge* (Art of the Fugue), Contrapunctus 12 (Rectus)

6.

Bach *Die Kunst der Fuge,* Contrapunctus 12 (Inversus)

E Ensembles—Two Voices: P5, P4, M3, and m3 within the Tonic Triad and M2 and m2

Follow the procedures given for unit 1E.

Unit 4

A Rhythm—Simple Meter: Quadruple Subdivision of the Beat

Section 1. Modules in Simple Meter

Using rhythm syllables or a neutral syllable, sing each of the given modules. Begin by repeating each module several times. Then treat the successive modules as a continuous exercise.

In these modules, you are subdividing the beat into four parts, representing the next logical ordering of the beat in the hierarchy of simple meter.

Rhythm Syllables

Select one of the following two systems if your instructor recommends you do so.

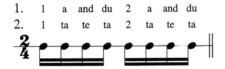

1.   1   a   and du   2   a   and du
2.   1   ta   te   ta   2   ta   te   ta

Some illustrations:

1.   1   du   2   3   1   du   2   and   1   an   du   2   a   and   3
2.   1   ta   2   3   1   ta   2   te   1   te   ta   2   ta   te   3

Section 2. Phrases in Simple Meter with Quadruple Division of the Beat

For numbers 1–5, follow the procedures outlined in unit 1A, section 2. For the two-part exercises (6–8), follow the procedures outlined in unit 2A, section 2.

8. Rhythmic framework for Jamaican Folksong

See unit 4E, exercise 9

Section 3. Creating a Coherent Phrase in Simple Meter

Return to section 1 and select four modules in the same meter. Place them in an order that would create a coherent four-measure phrase. Here is an example:

B Diatonic Models and Melodic Fragments for Interval Singing: m10, P8, P5, P4, M3, m3, M2, and m2

Section 1. Diatonic Models

These models anticipate the melodic fragments in the next section.

(a) Intervals Outlining the Tonic Triad and Dominant 7th Chord

Use an A major vocalise as a warm-up. For extra practice, sing this model in each of the major keys, using the last note of the pattern as the first note of the same pattern transposed a 4th lower or a 5th higher. See the following model:

(b) Intervals Emphasizing the Intervals P4 and P5, Filling in an Octave

For extra practice, this model can be repeated in all the minor keys by singing the pattern down a P5 (or up a P4) through all twelve keys. See the following model:

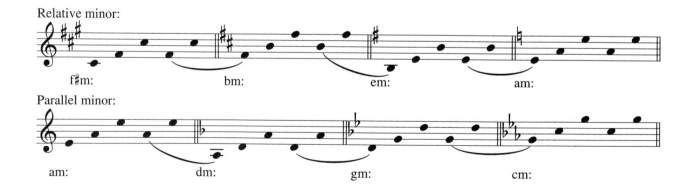

(c) Intervals of the P5, P4, M3, and m3, Filling in an Octave

For extra practice, this model may be repeated in all minor keys by singing the pattern down a P5 (up a P4).

Relative minor:

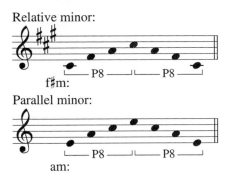

f♯m:

Parallel minor:

am:

(d) Intervals of the m10, P4, M3, and m3 Outlining the Tonic Triad

This model provides an unusual example of a tonic triad because the interval of a m10 occurs between the root and the 3rd. For extra practice, repeat this pattern in all minor keys.

Relative minor:

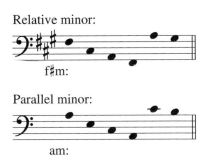

f♯m:

Parallel minor:

am:

Section 2. Melodic Fragments in A Major (F♯ Minor and A Minor)

1.   **Allegro**   Mozart *Eine kleine Nachtmusik* (A Little Night Music), K. 525 (transposed)

2a.   **Allegro con brio**   Wagner *Die fliegende Holländer* (The Flying Dutchman), Overture (first theme transposed)

3a.   **Allegro**   Schubert Symphony no. 5, Minuet (transposed)

4a.   **Allegro assai**   Mozart *Idomeneo,* Act I, Aria (Electra) (transposed)

fp

2b.
Allegro con brio

Wagner *Die fliegende Holländer,* Overture (first theme transposed)

3b.
Allegro

Schubert Symphony no. 5, Minuet (transposed)

4b. Allegro assai

Mozart *Idomeneo,* Act I, Aria (Electra) (transposed)

fp

Section 3. Creating a Coherent Melody

Return to section 2 and select two or three segments of melodic fragments that would create a coherent melody. It may be necessary to change the meter and rhythm of certain segments, depending on your choice. Here is an example based on measures 1 and 2 of fragment 2a, measures 2 and 3 of fragment 3a, and measure 4 of fragment 2a.

C Melodies (Major and Minor): P5, P4, M3, m3, M2, and m2

These melodies are limited to the same skips as those in unit 3C except that the skips may occur between scale degrees other than 1-3-5.

Melodies 1–3 are in major and include **calypso** rhythm patterns, introduced in part A of this unit (modules 26–41). All other melodies are in minor and utilize rhythm patterns introduced in previous units.

Melodies 4–12 are in minor and are taken from a publication entitled *Selected Jewish Songs* (for members of the armed forces, published by the National Jewish Welfare Board in cooperation with American Association for Jewish Education, copyright 1942, Jewish Welfare Board, member agency USO).

Follow the directions as outlined in unit 3C.

1.

Jestingly

Ratta Madan Law

(Ha   Ha)

(Ha   Ha)   (Ha   Ha)

See unit 4A, exercises 26–29

2.

Mattie Rag   (abridged)

See unit 4A, exercises 30–33, and unit 5B, section 2, exercise 8.

"Ratta Madan Law" and "Mattie Rag" from *Jamaica Land We Love* (Lloyd Hall). Macmillan Caribbean 1980.

3.

Back Down to the Tropics

Rhumba tempo

See unit 4A, exercises 38–41

"Back Down to the Tropics" Words and Music by Lionel Belasco and Leighla Whipper, from *Calypso Rhythm Songs*. Copyright © 1944 by Mills Music, Inc. 1619 Broadway.

4. Hevenu Shalom Aleychem

With spirit

5. Adon Olam

Moderato

6. Hin'ni Muchan Um'zuman

7. L'cha Dodi

8. Praise to the Living God—Yigdal

9. Yismach Moshe

D.C. al Fine

10. Ets Chayim Hi

11. Sim Shalom

12. Hasivenu Elecha

With abandon

D   Melodies (Major and Minor): P5, P4, M3, m3, M2, and m2

These melodies are limited to the same skips as those of unit 3C, except that the skips may occur between scale degrees other than 1-3-5.

Section 1. Schubert Songs

All melodies in this section are excerpted from the songs of Franz Schubert. Nearly all the rhythm patterns in these songs were already presented, except for the simple triplet in numbers 6 and 9; the three notes of the triplet should be spaced evenly over one complete beat.

5.   Schubert   *Der Leiermann* (The Organ Grinder) from *Winterreise,* op. 89, no. 24, D. 911

6.   Schubert   *Der Lindenbaum* (The Linden Tree) from *Winterreise,* op. 89, no. 5, D. 911

7.   Schubert   *Drang in die Ferne* (Urge to Roam), D. 770

8.   Schubert   *Der Musensohn* (The Son of the Muses), D. 764a

9.   Schubert   *Zwei Szenen aus "Lacrimas"* II (Delphine), op. 124, no. 1, D. 857 (2)

Section 2. Clef Reading

This section contains excerpts from the first movement of Schubert's Unfinished Symphony.

Procedures

1. Example 1 consists of the opening melody (mm. 13–20), played in unison by two oboes and two clarinets in A. To sing the clarinet part as it sounds, try to think in the soprano clef, with c' (middle C) on the bottom line. Experiment by using letter names and by checking your accuracy with the oboe part. Remember that the oboe is a nontransposing instrument and sounds the same pitches as the clarinet in A.

2. Example 2, from the same movement (mm. 291–298), also features different instruments playing melodies at the same pitch: violas (Vla) and cellos (Vc). Because these instruments are nontransposing, it is not necessary for you to use clefs for the purpose of changing key. Cello parts are sometimes written in the tenor clef but most often in the bass clef.

3. In this excerpt, the same melodic figure appears four times. For the purposes of this exercise, it is advised to consider the following temporary tonic pitches:

mm. 291–292—F♯ minor
mm. 293–294—E major
mm. 295–296—C♯ minor
mm. 297–298—B major

1.

Schubert   Symphony no. 8 (unfinished), D. 759, B Minor, I (mm. 13–20)

2.

Schubert   Symphony no. 8 (unfinished), D. 759, B Minor, I (mm. 291–298)

E Ensembles—Two Voices:
P5, P4, M3, m3, M2, and m2

The first eight excerpts are from chorale melodies harmonized by Bach. The ninth excerpt represents the outer voices of a Jamaican folk song. The rhythmic framework for this excerpt was presented in part A, section 2, number 8, of this unit. A tempo of ♩ = 72–80 is suggested for all examples.

Follow the procedures outlined in unit 1E, for **ensemble** singing.

#152* *Meinen Jesum laß' ich nicht, weil* (I Will Not Leave My Jesus)   #163 *Für Freuden laßt uns springen* (Let Us Leap with Joy)

#161 *Ihr Gestirn', ihr hohlen Lüfte* (Ye Stars, Ye Airy Winds)   #164 *Herr Gott, dich loben alle wir* (Lord God, We All Praise Thee)

#245 *Christe, der du bist Tag und Licht* (Christ, Who Art Day and Light)   #246 *Singt dem Herrn ein neues Lied*
(Sing the Lord a New Song)

#91 *Verleih' uns Frieden gnädiglich* (Mercifully Grant Us Peace) #198 *Christus, der uns selig macht* (Christ, Who Makes Us Blessed)

* These are Riemenschneider numbers.

9. **With disdain**

bass line adapted

See unit 4A, section 2, exercise 8

"Big, Big Sambo Gal" from *Jamaica Land We Love* (Lloyd Hall) Macmillan Caribbean 1980.

Unit 5

A Rhythm—Simple Meter: Irregular Division of the Beat (the Triplet)

Section 1. Modules in Simple Meter

Using rhythm syllables or a neutral syllable, sing each of the given modules. Begin by repeating each module several times. Then treat the successive modules as a continuous exercise.

In these modules, we are introducing the **triplet,** which represents an irregular division of the beat in simple meter. For a useful chart that shows the differences between regular and irregular divisions and subdivisions of the beat, see Benward and White, *Music in Theory and Practice,* vol. 1 (6th ed.), figure 1.19, p. 16.

Rhythm Syllables

Select one of the following two systems if your instructor recommends you do so.

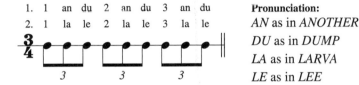

1. 1   an   du   2   an   du   3   an   du
2. 1   la   le   2   la   le   3   la   le

Pronunciation:
AN as in *ANOTHER*
DU as in *DUMP*
LA as in *LARVA*
LE as in *LEE*

Some illustrations:

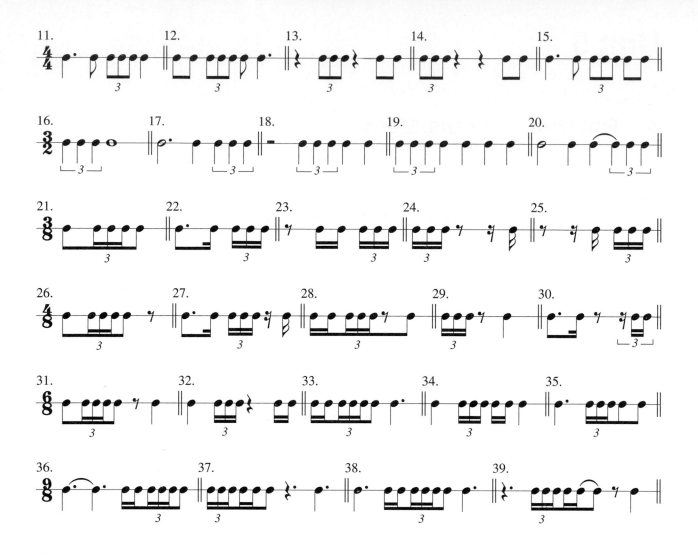

Section 2. Phrases in Simple Meter with Irregular Division of the Beat (the Triplet)

For numbers 1–5, follow the procedures outlined in unit 1A, section 2. For the two-part exercises (6–7), follow the procedures outlined in unit 2A, section 2.

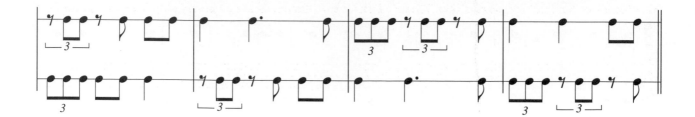

Section 3. Creating a Coherent Phrase in Simple Meter with a Triplet as an Example of an Irregular Division of the Beat

Return to section 1 and select three or four rhythm modules. Place them in an order that would create a coherent four-measure phrase. Because this procedure is clear, no example is provided here.

Write your solution on the following line:

B Diatonic Models and Melodic Fragments for Interval Singing—New Intervals: M6 and m6

Section 1. Diatonic Models

These models anticipate the melodic fragments in the next section.

These exercises emphasize intervals of the major 6th (M6) from scale degree 5 (C) in an ascending motion to scale degree 3 (A) before moving in a descending motion to scale degree 1 (F). Follow the same procedure as in previous units. For extra practice, sing these exercises in all major keys, transposing to each new key by P5s down or P4s up.

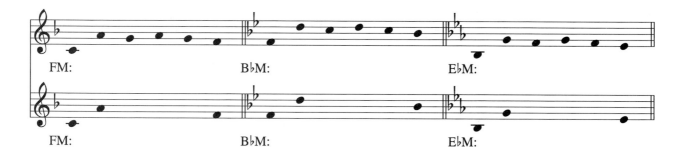

This model opens with the ascending M6 from scale degree 5 (C) up to scale degree 3 (A) and continues in an ascending motion to scale degree 1 (F).

Here the minor 6th (m6) is a chordal skip. The m6 (F down to A) functions as a consonant skip in support of the final pitch, C.

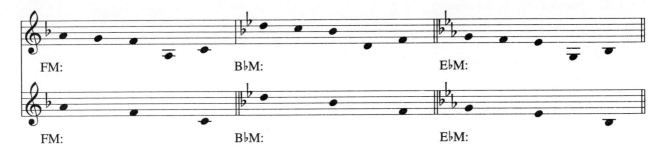

FM: BbM: EbM:

FM: BbM: EbM:

In this set, the major 6th (M6) is part of III in pure (natural minor).

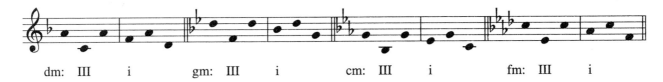

dm: III   i   gm: III   i   cm: III   i   fm: III   i

The sequential relationship of these exercises (F major) with triads on F and D is similar to that of the previous example, except that the tonic of the previous exercise is D minor. Use the same procedures as earlier.

FM: BbM: EbM:

These exercises outline the D-minor tonic triad. In this section, which serves as preparation for the singing of the melodic fragments, the authors recommend drills in relative minor rather than parallel minor because of the tonal design of melodic fragments 4 and 5, which begin in F major and end in D minor.

dm: gm: cm:

The last exercise introduces the M6 as a descending pattern from scale degree 3 (A) to scale degree 5 (C), first as part of a triadic pattern and then in combination with a m6 from scale degree 6 (D) to scale degree 4 (Bb).

FM: BbM: EbM:

Section 2. Melodic Fragments in F Major (and D minor)

1. Chopin   Nocturne, op. 9, no. 2 (transposed)

2. Chopin   Nocturne, op. 62, no. 2 (transposed)

3. Chopin   Nocturne, op. 27, no. 2 (transposed)

4. Chopin   Nocturne, op. 15, no. 3 (transposed)

5. Chopin   Nocturne, op. 55, no. 2 (transposed)

6. Chopin   Etude, op. 10, no. 9 (transposed)

7. Jamaica   "Mattie walla lef"

8. Jamaica   "Mattie Rag" (transposed)

See unit 4C, exercise 2.

Section 3. Creating a Coherent Melody

Return to section 2 and select two or three segments of melodic fragments that would create a coherent melody. It may be necessary to change the meter and rhythm of certain segments, depending on your choice.

Section 4. Practice in Clef Reading

Return to the melodic fragments in unit 1B, for practice in clef reading. To show your versatility, substitute the alto clef for the treble clef and change the key signature. See the following example:

C Melodies (Major and Minor)—New Intervals: M6 and m6

The next six songs are from a collection entitled *Six Creole Folk-Songs* (music arranged and translations by Maud Cuney Hare). Some of the rhythm and melodic fragments found in these songs emphasize the models of parts A and B of this unit.

1. Aurore Pradère (A Love Song)

2. Gardé piti mulet là (Musieu Bainjo) (Satirical Song)

3. Belle Layotte (A Love Song)

4. Quand mo-té jeune (Bal fini) (Dance song)

5. Aine, dé, trois, Caroline (Song of Longing)

6. Dialogue d'Amour (Song of Mockery)

D Melodies (Major and Minor)—New Intervals: M6 and m6

The format of this section resembles that of part B ("Diatonic Models and Melodic Fragments for Interval Singing") in that selected melodies are written in or transposed to the same key. Here, the melodies are in either G major or E minor. Because of the nature of these songs, it is an advantage to study them within the framework of the same key signature. For example, the key signature of E minor helps clarify the similarity between melodic patterns in two selections that are in natural minor: number 2, "Monday, Tuesday," from Ireland, and number 3, "The Laughter of Raindrops," from Jamaica. The modal flavor of the **subtonic** triad (D, F♯, A) in relation to the **tonic** triad (E, G, B) provides the link of continuity between these songs. In this section, some of the major melodies tilt toward relative minor and some of the minor melodies toward relative major.

1. Joe Primrose   St. James Infirmary (abridged)
Moderato

Mournfully

2. Traditional   Southern Counties, Ireland   *Da Luain, da Mairt* (Monday, Tuesday) (transposed)
Larghetto ♩. = 60

3. Kathleen McFarlane (Jamaica)   The Laughter of Raindrops (abridged)

"The Laughter of Raindrops" Music by Kathleen McFarlane, Words by Lisa Salmon. In *Jamaica, Land We Love* (Collection) Lloyd Hall. Macmillan Caribbean 1980

4. **Lent, avec grace** (♩. = 60)

Frantz Casséus   *Nan fond bois* (Far in the Woods) (abridged)

"Nan Fond Bois" (Far In the Woods) words and music by Frantz Casséus. G. Ricordi & Co., N.Y., 1961 #2193–3

5. **Bold with well defined rhythm**

Kathleen McFarlane (Jamaica)   (abridged) (transposed)

"Henry Morgan" words by W. Adolphe Roberts, Music by Kathleen McFarlane from *Jamaica, Land We Love,* Lloyd Hall. Macmillan Caribbean, 1980.

12.

"Cudelia Brown," #16, pp. 57–58 *Jamaica, Land We Love*, Lloyd Hall. Macmillan Caribbean, 1980.

E Ensembles

This unit closes with works that require accompaniment. The first is entitled "Mon Coeur est en Peine," which is described as "Chanson à plusieurs voix, avec orchestre de Valihas." In translation, this means that the song is for several voices with an orchestra of valihas. The **valiha** is described in the *Grove Dictionary of Musical Instruments* (vol. 3, p. 705) as "The name commonly used in Madagascar for the **tube zither.** The valiha is one of the oldest Malagasy instruments, originating in Southeast Asia, and it has become the symbol of cultural unity in the island" (emphasis added). The accompaniment and text are provided.

The second work is entitled "He's Worthy to Be Praised" (words and music by Tony Leach and dedicated to the St. Paul Baptist Church, Harrisburg, Pennsylvania). The accompaniment and text are provided.

Mon cœur est en pei - ne.

Mon cœur est en pei - ne.

Bien lourde est ma chaî - ne.

Bien lourde est ma chaî - ne.

Men-ez-moi chez moi, mon cœur est a - gi - té.

Men-ez-moi,   Ra - me - nez-moi,   mon cœur est trou-blé.   De cha-grin

De cha-grin mon âme est af - fli - gé - e.   Mon   cœur est en

mon   âme   est   af - fli - gé - e.   Mon   cœur   est   en

pei - ne.   Bien   dure   est ma chaî - ne

pei - ne.   Bien   dure   est ma chaî - ne

De cha-grin mon âme est af - fli - gé - e.

De cha-grin mon âme est af - fli - gé - e.

Mais main-te-nant elle é-cla-te de joi - e

Mais main-te-nant elle é-cla-te de joi - e

Ma bien ai-mée a pa-ru sur ma voi - e

Hé hé, mes a -

Ma bien ai-mée a pa-ru sur ma voi - e

mours   El - le res-sem-ble à l'oi-seau qui se po - se

El - le res-sem-ble à l'oi-seau qui se po - se

Je   ne veux pas que se fa-ne la ro - se   De la voir l'es-poir à moi s'im-

Je   ne veux pas que se fa-ne la ro - se.

po - se   Mon

bien chanté   Mon

coeur est en pei-ne — Bien lourde est ma chaî-ne

coeur est en pei-ne — Bien lourde est ma chaî-ne

Oui, d'a - mour mon â-me est plei-ne.

Oui, d'a - mour mon âme est plei-ne.

2.

Lord for He's wor - thy to be praised!

"He's Worthy to be Praised" Words and Music by Tony Leach. Copyright 1996 by Tony Leach, Penn State School of Music, University Park, PA, 16802.

Unit 6

A   Rhythm—Simple Meter: More Difficult Quadruple Subdivision of the Beat

Section 1. Modules in Simple Meter

Using rhythm syllables or a neutral syllable, sing each of the given modules. Begin by repeating each module several times. Then treat the successive modules as a continuous exercise.

Just as in the modules of unit 4, we are subdividing the beat into four parts which represents the next logical ordering of the beat in the hierarchy of simple meter.

Rhythm Syllables

Select one of the two systems illustrated in unit 4A, if your instructor recommends you do so.

See unit 6A, section 2, exercise 9.

Section 2. Phrases in Simple Meter

2. Rhythmic crescendo and decrescendo

5.

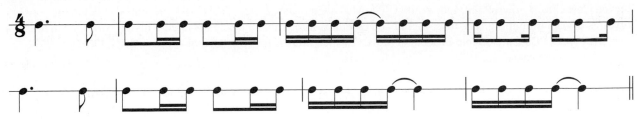

6. Alternating $\frac{2}{4}$ and $\frac{3}{4}$; see "The Raftsman's Song," in this unit

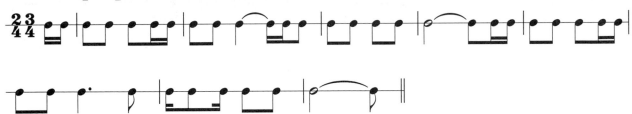

7. The upper voice is a rhythmic augmentation of the first four bars of the lower voice.

8. Rhythmic ostinato

Adapted from *The Music of Santería,* pp. 109–110. *Traditional Rhythms of the Batá Drums,* by John Amira and Steven Cornelius (Crown Point, Ind. White Cliffs Media Company, 1992). "This book presents the salute (or praise) rhythms of batá drumming. The most sacred and complex of the ritual music associated with the Afro-Cuban religion Santería" (p.1). "Batá are double-headed, hourglass shaped drums" (p. 15). "Ochún—a river deity, Ochún is the goddess of love and beauty" (p. 109).

9.   Ochún

Section 3. Creating a Coherent Phrase in Simple Meter

Return to section 1 and select three or four rhythm modules. Place them in an order that would create a coherent four-measure phrase.

Write your solution on the following line:

B Diatonic Models and Melodic Fragments for Interval Singing—Review: M6 and m6

Section 1. Diatonic Models

These models anticipate the melodic fragments in the next section.

These exercises emphasize intervals of the chordal skips within a major tonic triad starting with the root, moving down to the 5th and then up to the 3rd. The upward skip from scale degree 5 to scale degree 3 results in the interval of a major 6th (M6). Follow the same procedure as in previous units. For extra practice, sing these exercises in all major keys, transposing to each new key by P5s down or P4s up. The tossing of triads among students should continue, as shown in the following model:

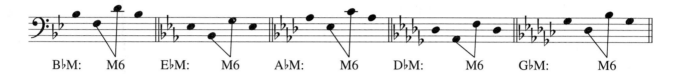

The first three melodic fragments (Mozart, Beethoven, and Makeba) follow a similar melodic contour.

These exercises emphasize the chordal skips within a major tonic triad, starting with the root, moving to the 3rd, and then down to the 5th. The downward skip from scale degree 3 to scale degree 5 results in a major 6th (M6). Follow the same procedures as in previous units. Sing the model in all major keys, transposing in the manner described in each previous unit.

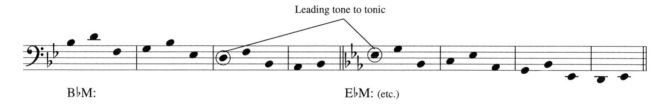

The tonic and subdominant triads are outlined. The dominant is implied only with the leading tone as it progresses to tonic.

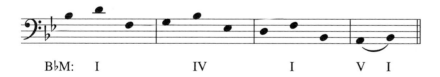

These exercises combine the major and minor 6th patterns that form the basis of melodic fragments 5, 6, and 7. Follow the same procedure as described in previous units, using the following model as the basis for transposition.

This model emphasizes the ascending major 6th (M6), followed by a descending scale line, and may be thought of in B♭ major as well as G minor. This exercise is related to fragments 8–10.

Section 2. Melodic Fragments in B♭ major (B♭ Minor and G Minor)

1. Mozart   Requiem, K. 626, *Tuba Mirum*

2. Beethoven   *Fidelio* (Overture), op. 72C (transposed and adapted)

3. African Folk Song   *Dubula* (Shoot) (transposed) *(Makeba)*

4. Mozart   Minuet, K. 2, no. 2 (transposed)

5. Musorgsky   *Boris Godounov* (Opera), Scene 2 (transposed)

6a. Mozart   *Requiem,* K. 626, Lacrymosa (Tears)

6b. Mozart   *Requiem,* K. 626, Lacrymosa (Tears) (transposed)

7a. Schubert Variation on a Waltz by Diabelli, D. 718

7b. Schubert Variation on a Waltz by Diabelli, D. 718 (transposed)

8. Tchaikovsky Symphony no. 5, op. 64 (transposed)

9. Mozart Six German Dances, no. v, K. 509 (transposed)

10. Mahler *Wer hat dies Liedlein erdacht* (Up There on the Hill) from *Des Knaben Wunderhorn* (The Youth's Magic Horn) (transposed)

Section 3. Creating a Coherent Melody

Return to section 2 and select two or three segments of melodic fragments that would create a coherent melody. It may be necessary to change the meter and rhythm of certain segments, depending on your choice.

Section 4. Practice in Clef Reading: Alto Clef

Return to the melodic fragments of unit 2B for practice in clef reading. Substitute the alto clef for the treble clef and change the key signature.

C Melodies (Major and Minor): M6 and m6

The six songs in this section include folk songs from the northern woods of the United States; the cities of Basel and Lausanne, Switzerland; and Tahiti. Some of the rhythm and melodic fragments found in these songs emphasize the models of parts A and B of this unit.

1. I Am a River Driver

"I Am a River Driver" p. 203 from *Lumbering Songs from the Northern Woods* by Edith Fowke, Tunes Transcribed by Norman Cazden. Published for the American Folklore Society by the University of Texas Press, Austin and London: copyright 1970 by the American Folklore Society Memoir Series Wm. Hugh Jansen, General Editor, Vol. 55, 1970.

2. How We Got Up to the Woods Last Year

"How We Got Up to the Woods Last Year", p. 162 from *Lumbering Songs from the Northern Woods* by Edith Fowke, Tunes Transcribed by Norman Cazden. Published for the American Folklore Society by the University of Texas Press, Austin and London: copyright 1970 by the American Folklore Society Memoir Series Wm. Hugh Jansen, General Editor, Vol. 55, 1970.

3. The Raftsmen's Song

"The Raftsmen's Song", p. 212 from *Lumbering Songs from the Northern Woods* by Edith Fowke, Tunes Transcribed by Norman Cazden. Published for the American Folklore Society by the University of Texas Press, Austin and London: copyright 1970 by the American Folklore Society Memoir Series Wm. Hugh Jansen, General Editor, Vol. 55, 1970.

4. *Z'Basel an mym Rhy*

5. *Voici la mi-ete*

6. *Adieux a Taïti*

Souple et modéré

D Melodies (Major and Minor): M6 and m6

Section 1. Robert Schumann

The melodies in this section are taken from instrumental works by Robert Schumann. The first two selections from Schumann's *Album for the Young*, op. 68, provide further exercises in clef reading.

Example 1: This excerpt is in A B A form. The melody of the B section is the same as A except that it centers around G as tonic rather than C. With the return of the original material in the final A, the bass clef is used to illustrate the 5th relationship between the bass and tenor clefs.

Example 2: Line 2 is almost identical to line 1, except for its octave transposition, and allows you to check to see whether you are reading the clef correctly. The only new clef is the mezzo-soprano clef, which places middle C (c') on the second line up from the lowest.

1.

Schumann *Trällerliedchen* (Humming Tune), op. 68, no. 3

Nicht schnell

(Sing this line an octave higher)

2.

Schumann *Wilder Reiter* (The Mad Horseman), op. 68, no. 8

The clef reading strategies outlined for examples 1 and 2 should be applied to melodies 3–10, also by Schumann.

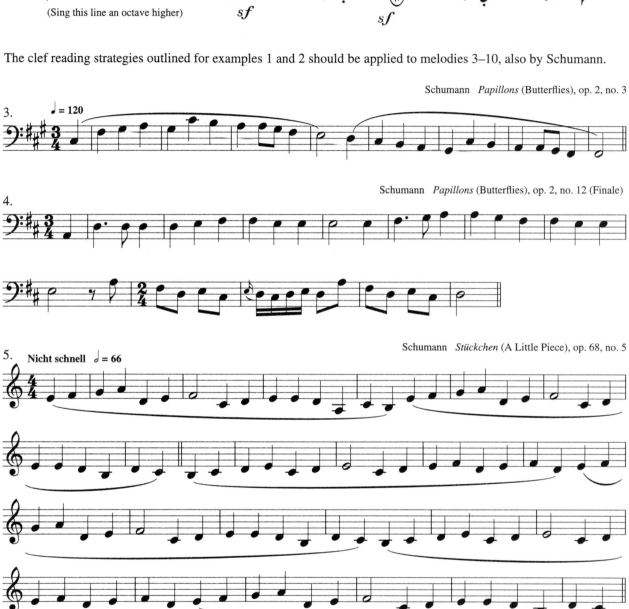

Schumann *Papillons* (Butterflies), op. 2, no. 3

3.

Schumann *Papillons* (Butterflies), op. 2, no. 12 (Finale)

4.

Schumann *Stückchen* (A Little Piece), op. 68, no. 5

5.

6.

Schumann   #5 from *Albumblätter* (Album Leaves), op. 99, no. 8

Schumann   *Scherzo* op. 99, no. 13

Schumann   *Kleine Romanze* (Little Romance), op. 68, no. 19 (transposed) (abridged)

Schumann   *Ernteliedchen* (Harvest Song), op. 68, no. 24 (transposed) (abridged)

Schumann   *Schnitterliedchen* (The Reapers' Song), op. 68, no. 18

Section 2. From Bach to Barber

The six melodies in this section are from works by various composers from Bach to Barber.

Transpose this familiar Rossini tune up a minor 2nd to F major, starting on note C, by reading in the alto clef (displaced by an octave).

1.   Rossini   William Tell Overture, R-10

Allegro vivace

ff

* Ten measures omitted

pp

Schubert   *Ecossaise* I, D. 421

2.

*f

(mm. 1–4) * octave lower than original

3.   Bach   English Suite III, Gavotte II (or Musette)

*(eight measures omitted)

4.   Bach   Brandenburg Concerto no. 2, I (transposed down two octaves)

5. **In waltz time** ♩ = 112

"Under The Willow Tree" from *Vanessa* by Samuel Barber. Copyright © 1952 (Renewed) by G. Schirmer, Inc. (ASCAP) International copyright Secured. All rights reserved. Reprinted by permission of G. Schirmer, Inc.

6. **Andante, un poco moso** ♩ = 96

"Bessie Bobtail" Op. 2, No. 3 by Samuel Barber. Copyright © 1936 (Renewed) by G. Schirmer, Inc. (ASCAP)   International Copyright Secured. All Rights Reserved. Reprinted by Permission.

E Ensembles

The first ensemble excerpt in this unit is from the same collection as that of unit 5E. This ensemble is abridged from number 8 (pp. 23–24 and 26–27) in volume 3 (Aux îles des mers lointaines) of Chansons nègres, recueillies, traduites et harmonisées par Julien Tiersot (copyright 1933 Heugel Editeur, Paris). The other excerpts are from works by Bartók, Beethoven, and Mozart.

1.

Un peu animé

Ronde des Enfants au Clair de Lune (abridged)

mf

Au clair de la lu - ne   Au clair de la

Hé hé hé hé

2 voix ad lib.

lu - ne   Bien tôt se lè - ve l'au-ro - re

Hé hé hé hé

Soy - ez bien ven-us, en - fants, Dan - sez

a o a o ____

Ki - tsa-o tsa-ho ho ho

Bartók *Mikrokosmos, Vol. II (Méditation)*

2. **Andante** (♩ = 86)

mf

p

p

mf

Béla Bartók, *Mikrokosmos,* Vol. II (Meditation). From *Rumanian Folk Dances.* © Copyright 1940 by Hawkes & Son (London) Ltd. Copyright Renewed. Definitive corrected edition © Copyright 1987 by Hawkes & Son (London) Ltd. Reprinted by permission of Boosey & Hawkes, Inc.

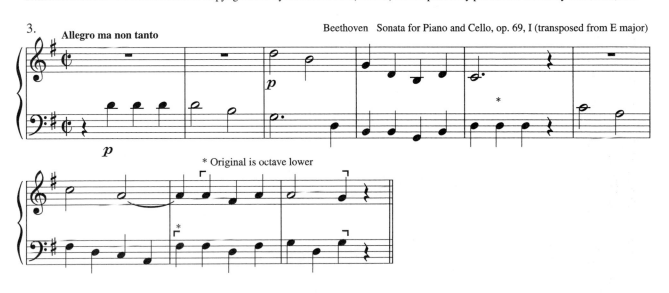

3. **Allegro ma non tanto**

Beethoven Sonata for Piano and Cello, op. 69, I (transposed from E major)

p

*

* Original is octave lower

*

4.

Unit 7

A Rhythm—Review of Simple Meter with Emphasis on Irregular Division of the Beat: The Triplet

Section 1. Modules in Simple Meter

Using rhythm syllables or a neutral syllable, sing each of the given modules. Begin by repeating each module several times. Then treat the successive modules as a continuous exercise.

Just as in the modules of unit 5, we are emphasizing the **triplet,** which represents an irregular division of the beat in simple meter.

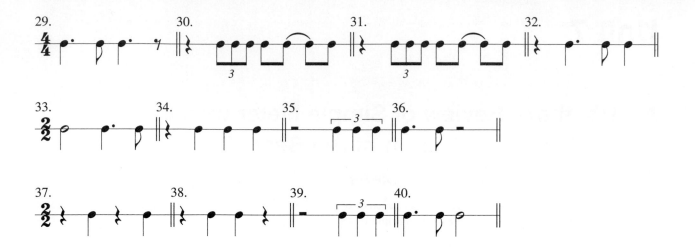

Section 2. Phrases in Simple Meter with Irregular Division of the Beat: The Triplet

For numbers 1–4, follow the procedures outlined in unit 1A, section 2. For the two-part exercises (5–6), follow the procedures outlined in unit 2A, section 2.

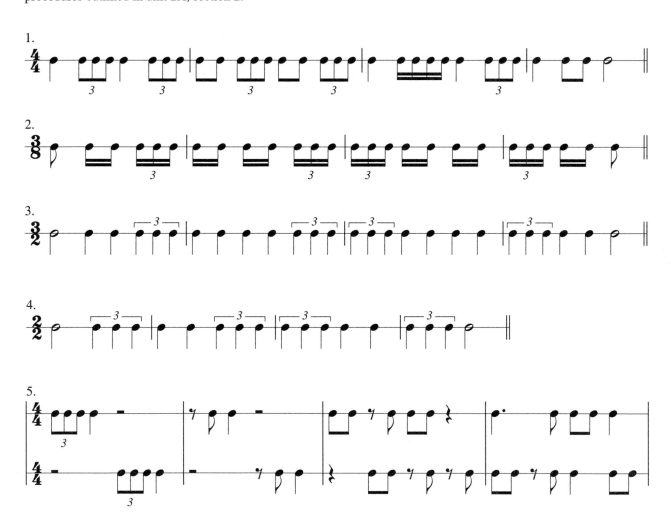

6. Rhythmic canon

This ensemble passage is taken from a larger work entitled "Quitta Mouille" for two drums and is representative of Haitian drumming. For further information, see "Drum Music for Two Dances," chapter 7 in *Haiti Singing,* by Harold Courlander (Chapel Hill: University of North Carolina Press, 1939).

Quitta Mouille

Section 3. Creating a Coherent Phrase in Simple Meter

Return to section 1 and select three or four rhythm modules. Place them in an order that would create a coherent four-measure phrase.

Write your solution on the following line:

B   Diatonic Models and Melodic Fragments for Interval Singing—New Interval: m7

Section 1. Diatonic Models

The exercises in this section relate to the music of Haydn, Mozart, and Beethoven, with particular emphasis on the minor 7th. The musical fragments that correspond with these exercises are quoted in section 2.

The two models that follow are related to the Haydn and Mozart fragments (nos. 1 and 2). Treat these models as exercises in antiphonal singing by having half the class sing "a" and the other half answer by singing "b." Continue this process in all major keys, transposing to each new key by P5s down or P4s up.

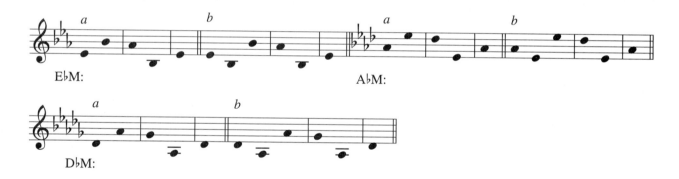

Follow the same principle of antiphonal singing with the next model. Letter "a" represents fragment 3 (Mozart's Horn Concerto, K. 447, first movement); "b" represents fragment 4 from the third movement of the same concerto.

Here is another model for antiphonal singing. Letter "a" corresponds with fragment 5 (from the second movement of the same horn concerto as fragments 3 and 4); "b" corresponds with fragment 6 from another Mozart Horn Concerto (K. 447, second movement).

This model follows the contour of fragment 7 (Haydn) and fragment 8 (Beethoven). Sing the model in all major keys.

The last three melodic fragments (9, 10, and 11) in the next section are further illustrations of the patterns already presented.

E♭M: 8va   A♭M: 8va   D♭M: 8va

Section 2. Melodic Fragments in E♭ Major

1. Haydn Symphony no. 94 (second movement–transposed)

2. Mozart *Eine kleine Nachtmusik* (A Little Night Music), K. 525 (transposed)

3. Mozart Horn Concerto, K. 447 (first movement)

4. Mozart Horn Concerto, K. 447 (third movement)

5. Mozart Horn Concerto, K. 447 (second movement–transposed)

6. Mozart Horn Concerto, K. 495 (second movement–adapted)

7. Haydn Symphony no. 88 (second movement–transposed)

8. Beethoven op. 10, no. 1 (first movement)

Allegro molto e con brio

9. Beethoven Piano Concerto no. 5, op. 73 (second movement)

Adagio un poco moso (♩ = 60)

10. Beethoven String Quartet, op. 18, no. 3 (transposed)

Allegro (♩ = 120)

11. Beethoven String Quartet, op. 18, no. 4

Allegro ma non Tanto (♩ = 84)

Section 3. Creating a Coherent Melody

Return to section 2 and select two or three segments of melodic fragments that would create a coherent melody. It may be necessary to change the meter and rhythm of certain segments, depending on your choice.

Section 4. Practice in Clef Reading: Alto Clef

Return now to the melodic fragments of unit 3 for practice in clef reading. Substitute the alto clef for the given clef and change the key signature.

C   Melodies (Major and Minor): M6 and m6

Section 1: Melodies from Songs and Instrumental Works by Beethoven

The melodies in this section are from instrumental and vocal works by Beethoven.

Beethoven   Two Sonatinas, I (transposed)

Beethoven   Two Sonatinas, I *Romanze* (transposed)

Beethoven   Three Sonatas, no. 3, II, Var. II, WoO 47

Beethoven   Three Sonatas, no.3, Var. VI, WoO 47

Beethoven *Urians Reise um die Welt* (Urian's Journey Round the World), op. 52, no. 1

5. **In einer massigen geschwinden Bewegung mit einer komischen Art gesungen**

Beethoven *Feuerfarb'* (Flame Color), op. 52, no. 2

6. **Andante con moto**

Beethoven *Das Glück der freundschaft* (The Joy of Friendship), op. 88

7. **Andante quasi allegretto**

Beethoven *Der Mann von Wort* (A Man of His Word), op. 99 (transposed)

8. **Gemäss dem verschiedenen Ausdruck in den Versen piano und forte**

Section 2. Short Melodies

These short melodies will provide the opportunity for rapid reading of melodic patterns that are typical of music of the common practice period.

D Melodies (Major and Minor): M6 and m6

The melodies in this section are taken from instrumental works by George Friedrich Händel. The HWV numbers are from the reference manual of the *Händel-Handbuch* (vol. 3), published by Bärenreiter Kassel, Basel and London, 1986.

1. Handel *Wassermusik* (Water Music), 12 Suite no. II, D Major *Alla Hornpipe*, HWV. 349 (transposed)

2. Handel *Wassermusik* (Water Music), 8 Suite no. I, F Major *Bourrée*, HWV. 348 (transposed)

3. Handel Suite no. 7, B-flat, *Gigue*, HWV. 440

4. Handel *Wassermusik* (Water Music), 4 Suite no. I, F Major, HWV. 348 (transposed)

5. Handel Suite no. 1 B-flat Major, *Menuet*, HWV. 434 (transposed 8ve lower)

6. Handel Suite no. 9 in G Major, *Chaconne*, HWV. 442 (transposed)

7. Handel   Suite no. 8 in G Major, *Gigue,* HWV. 441

8. Handel   Suite no. 3 in D Minor, Var. 4, HWV. 428

9. Handel   Suite no. 4 in D Minor, *Sarabande,* Var. 1, HWV. 437

10. Handel   Suite no. 5 in E Major, Air, "The Harmonious Black Smith," HWV. 430

E Ensembles

These excerpts are from works by Handel, Couperin, Haydn, and Bach.

1.

Handel   Suite no. 9, G Major, Var. 62, HWV. 442 (transposed)

2.

Couperin   *Les Moissonneurs* (The Reapers)

Gioioso

This is an interesting excerpt because, according to the directions, it may be sung forward and backward, then turned upside down and sung both forward and backward. The text translates freely: "You should dedicate yourself entirely to your art."

3.

Haydn

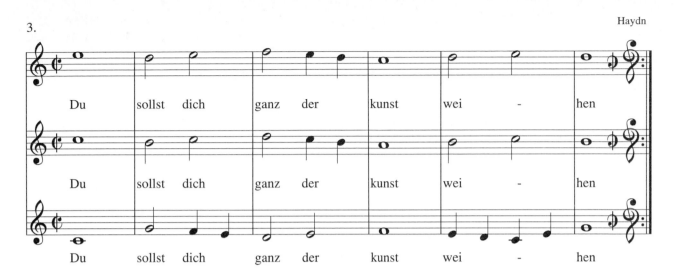

Du   sollst   dich   ganz   der   kunst   wei   -   hen

Du   sollst   dich   ganz   der   kunst   wei   -   hen

Du   sollst   dich   ganz   der   kunst   wei   -   hen

Transpose this familiar melody down a major 2nd to G by reading the upper line in tenor clef (for these purposes, the fourth line is c'', an 8ve higher than c') and the lower line in alto clef (for these purposes, the middle line is c, an 8ve lower than c').

4.

Bach   A canon from *In dulci jubilo* (In Sweet Jubilation), BWV 608 (double canon at 8ve)

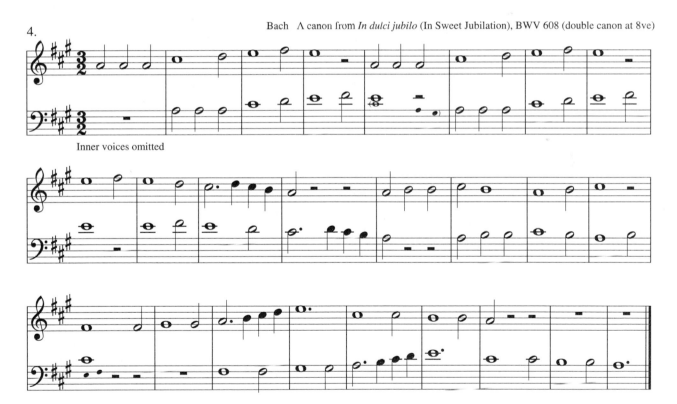

Inner voices omitted

Unit 8

A Rhythm—Review of Simple Meter and Compound Meter

Section 1. Modules in Simple Meter

Follow the procedures given in the previous units.

Section 2. Phrases in Compound Meter

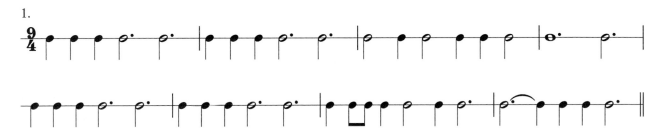

7.

Adapted from *The Music of Santería,* pp. 91–92. *Traditional Rhythms of the Bata Drums,* by John Amira and Steven Cornelius (Crown Point, Ind.: White Cliffs Media Company, 1992).

8.   Oricha Oko

Section 3. Creating a Coherent Phrase in Simple or Compound Meter

Return to section 1 and select three or four rhythm modules. Place them in an order that would create a coherent four-measure phrase.

Write your solution on the following line:

B Diatonic Models and Melodic Fragments for Interval Singing—New Interval: M7

Section 1. Diatonic Models

The exercises in this section relate to the music of Verdi, Stravinsky, Wagner, Bach, and Beethoven with particular emphasis on the minor 7th (m7). The musical fragments that correspond with these exercises are quoted in section 2.

The first model (in minor) is related to the first melodic fragment (Bach); the second model (in major) is related to fragments 2 and 3 by Wagner. Sing the first model in keys a minor 3rd above (i.e., c, e♭, f♯), then sing the next model in keys a minor 3rd below (E♭, C, A, and so on).

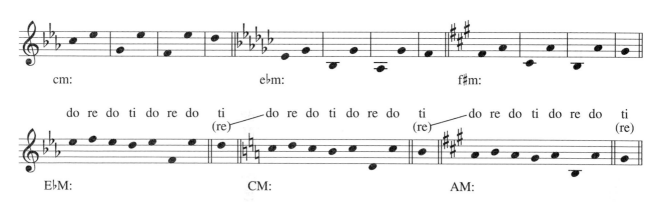

If you find it difficult to sing the second model in keys separated by a minor 3rd, the reason is that the melodic patterns combine to form a segment of the octatonic scale (i.e., a scale of alternating major and minor seconds). See the following model:

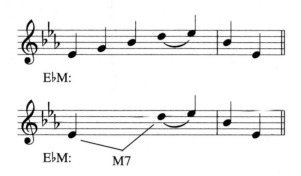

Only two models are necessary to introduce the major 7th (M7) from E♭ to D. These are preparatory materials for melodic fragments 5–7.

Only two models are necessary to introduce the major 7th (M7, from A♭ to G) as preparation for melodic fragments 8 and 9. The second model is almost the reverse of the first.

These models are quite similar to the previous two, except that they are in minor keys. For those who want to emphasize **relative** relationships, C minor is provided; for those who prefer **parallel** relationships, E♭ minor is available. These models are in preparation for melodic fragments 10, 10a, 11, and 11a in the next section.

Section 2. Melodic Fragments in C Minor, E♭ Major, and E♭ Minor

1. Bach   Partita no. 6, *Gavotte* (transposed)

2. Wagner   *The Twilight of the Gods,* Act III, Scene 3 (transposed)

3. Wagner   *The Twilight of the Gods,* Act III, Scene 1 (transposed)

4. Wagner   *The Twilight of the Gods,* Act III, Scene 2 (transposed)

5. Verdi   *Aida,* Act IV (transposed)

6. Stravinsky   *Petrushka* (transposed)

7. Beethoven   Piano Sonata, op. 10, no. 3 (first movement—transposed)

8. Bach   French Suite no. 6, *Allemande* (transposed)

9. Bach   Partita no. 2, *Rondeau*

10a. Bach French Suite no. 3, *Sarabande* (transposed)

10b. Bach French Suite no. 3, *Sarabande* (transposed)

11a. Bach *Well-Tempered Clavier,* Book I, Fugue 10 (transposed)

11b. Bach *Well-Tempered Clavier,* Book I, Fugue 10 (transposed)

12a. Bach *Die Kunst der Fuge* (Art of the Fugue), no. 9 (transposed)

12b. Bach *Die Kunst der Fuge,* no. 9 (transposed)

13a. Bach English Suite no. 5, *Gigue* (transposed)

13b. Bach English Suite no. 5, *Gigue* (transposed)

Section 3. Creating a Coherent Melody

Return to section 2 and select two or three segments of melodic fragments that would create a coherent melody. It may be necessary to change the meter and rhythm of certain segments, depending on your choice.

Section 4. Practice in Clef Reading: Alto Clef

Return now to the melodic fragments of unit 3 for practice in clef reading. Substitute the alto clef for the given clef and change the key signature.

C   Melodies (Major and Minor): m7

Section 1. Melodies from Operas by Verdi, Puccini, Handel, and Pergolesi

The melodies in this section are from operas by Verdi, Puccini, Handel, and Pergolesi.

10. **Allegro assai**

Uberto
Pandolphe

Section 2. Excerpts from Cantatas Written by J. S. Bach

The excerpts in this section are taken from the cantatas of J. S. Bach.

1. Cantata no. 4

2. Cantata no. 5

3. Cantata no. 46

4. Cantata no. 42

5. Cantata no. 72

6. Cantata no. 75

7. Cantata no. 89

8. Cantata no. 144

9. Cantata no. 189

10. Cantata no. 197

D Melodies (Major and Minor): m7

Section 1. Folk Songs from the U.S. Northern Woods and Haiti, Melodies from Instrumental Works by Bach and Bruckner

The first six melodies in this section are from folk song collections of the northern woods of the United States and of Haiti and emphasize some of the most complicated rhythm patterns presented thus far. The next six melodies are from the keyboard literature of Bach. The last 2 melodies are from Bruckner's Fifth Symphony, second movement.

The juxtaposition of the Bruckner excerpts with those from the *Art of the Fugue* in this section, as well as in the subsequent Part E, "Ensembles," gives evidence of Bruckner's homage to this monumental work by Bach.

1. Driving Saw-Logs on the Plover (dC 29)

"Driving Saw-Logs on the Plover" from *Lumbering Songs from the Northern Woods* by Edith Fowke, Tunes Transcribed by Norman Cazden. Published for the American Folklore Society by the University of Texas Press, Austin and London: copyright 1970 by the American Folklore Society Memoir Series Wm. Hugh Jansen, General Editor, Vol. 55, 1970.

2. Save Your Money While You're Young

Haitian Songs

"Save Your Money While You're Young" from *Lumbering Songs from the Northern Woods* by Edith Fowke, Tunes Transcribed by Norman Cazden. Published for the American Folklore Society by the University of Texas Press, Austin and London: copyright 1970 by the American Folklore Society Memoir Series Wm. Hugh Jansen, General Editor, Vol. 55, 1970.

Bach   Minuet I from *Drei Menuette aus dem Klavierbüchlein für W. F. Bach,* BWV 841

Bach   Overture in F Major, *Gigue,* BWV 820

Bach   Overture in F Major, *Trio,* BWV 820

Bach   Overture in F Major, *Bourrée,* BWV 820

Bach   *Die Kunst der Fuge* (Art of the Fugue), Contrapunctus XIII (Rectus)

Bach   *Die Kunst der Fuge,* Contrapunctus XIII (Inversus) (two octaves lower)

13. **Sehr langsam**
dolce

Bruckner   Symphony No. 5, ii

oboe

14. **Sehr langsam**

cello

E   Ensembles

1.

Haydn

Bach   *Die Kunst der Fuge,* Contrapunctus V

2.

Beethoven   WoO 50, II

3. **Allegretto**

* See unit 9B for d5.

Beethoven WoO 192

4. Voices

① ② ③ ④

Ars lon - ga, vi - ta bre - vis.

Beethoven WoO 193

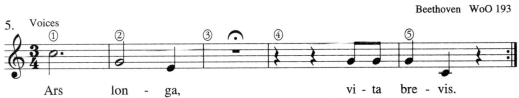

5. Voices

① ② ③ ④ ⑤

Ars lon - ga, vi - ta bre - vis.

Beethoven WoO 191

6. ① B - A - C - H

Kühl, — nicht lau, nicht lau, kühl, — nicht lau, kühl, — nicht lau.

② Kül, — nicht lau, kühl, — nicht lau, nicht lau.

③ Kühl, — nicht lau, kühl, — nicht lau, kühl, — nicht lau.

Unit 9

A Rhythm—Compound Meter: Subdivision of the Beat

Section 1. Modules in Compound Meter

Using rhythm syllables or a neutral syllable, sing each of the given modules. Begin by repeating each module several times. Then treat the successive modules as a continuous exercise.

Rhythm Syllables

Use the following syllables if your instructor recommends you do so.

Section 2. Phrases in Simple and Compound Meters with Triple Subdivisions

1.

2. Rhythmic crescendo and decrescendo

3.

4.

5.

6. Rhythmic canon

Section 3. Creating a Coherent Phrase in Compound Meter

Return to section 1 and select three or four rhythm modules. Place them in an order that would create a coherent four-measure phrase.

Write your solution on the following line:

B Diatonic Models and Melodic Fragments for Interval Singing—New Intervals: A4 and d5

Section 1. Diatonic Models

The exercises in this section relate to the melodic fragments of Bach, Beethoven, and Mozart.

The following examples emphasize the resolution of the diminished 5th (d5; D♯–A) to the major 3rd (M3; E–G♯), as given in the following model:

Learning to sing the exercises derived from this excerpt will help you understand the intricacies of voice leading involved in the treatment of tritones. Most often, successive melodic tritones are harmonized by dominant 7th chords, moving sequentially downward by P5s. Sing the following model in all major keys, transposing to each new key by P5s down or P4s up, as shown in the following model:

Try the following accelerated method for traveling through the various keys.

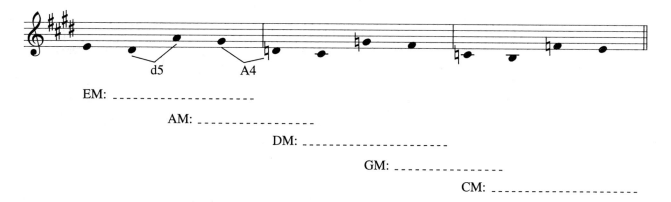

This model shows the resolution of the augmented 4th (A4; F♯–B♯) to the major 6th (M6; E–C♯) and is related to fragment 6.

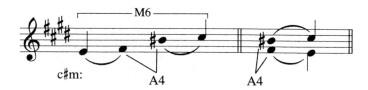

The next series of models (indicated as 7a–b–12a–b) relate to the Bach chorales in the next section. For those who are learning La-based minor, sing 7a–12a. If your instructor prefers Do-based minor, sing 7b–12b. If fixed La or chromatic fixed Do is the preference, you should sing both types of models (7a–12b).

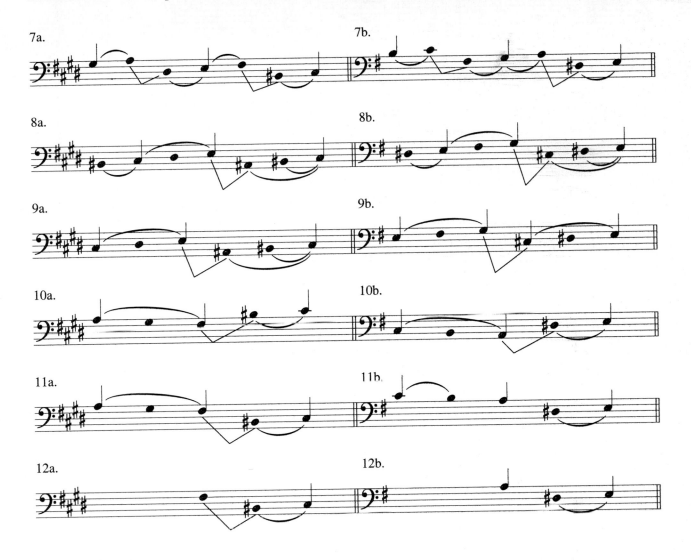

Section 2. Melodic Fragments in E Major (C# Minor and E Minor)

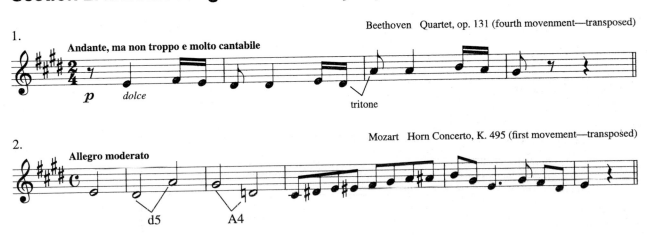

3. Beethoven Quartet, op. 130 (fourth movement—transposed)

4. Mozart Horn Concerto, K. 417 (third movement—transposed)

5. Beethoven Quartet, op. 135 (third movement)

6. Beethoven op. 131, no. 7

7a. Bach Chorale no. 78 (abridged and transposed)   7b.

8a. Bach Chorale no. 126 (transposed)   8b.

9a. Bach Chorale no. 134 (transposed)   9b.

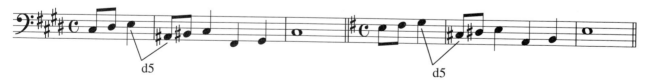

10a. Bach Chorale no. 170 (transposed)   10b.

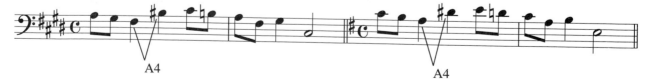

11a. Bach Chorale no. 178 (transposed)   11b.

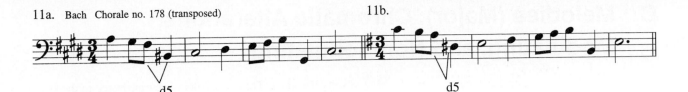

d5   d5

12a. Bach Chorale no. 172 (transposed and abridged)   12b.

d5   d5

Supplemental fragments emphasizing secondary leading-tone [LT] functions.

13. Beethoven Symphony no. 1, op. 21, I (m. 1–4 transposed from C major)

EM: d5   A4

14. Beethoven Symphony no. 1, op. 21 (mm. 41–45 abridged and transposed)

EM:

Section 3. Creating a Coherent Melody

Return to section 2 and select two or three segments of melodic fragments that would create a coherent melody. It may be necessary to change the meter and rhythm of certain segments, depending on your choice.

Section 4. Practice in Clef Reading: Alto Clef and Tenor Clef

Return to the melodic fragments of unit 5 for practice in clef reading. Substitute the alto clef for the treble clef and change the key signature.

Return to the melodic fragments of unit 1 for practice in clef reading. Substitute the tenor clef for the treble clef and change the key signature.

C Melodies (Major): Chromatic Alterations, Modulating, and Nonmodulating

The melodies in this section are excerpts from the Mozart song literature. These excerpts were transposed to the key of C major for ease in seeing and hearing notes outside the diatonic framework. Examples include alterations of the following scale degrees: 4 (F#), 2 (D#), 5 (G#), and 1 (C#). These exercises are designed to assist you with the Mozart songs in the next part of this unit.

1. Mozart *O Heiliges Band (der Freundschaft)* [O Holy Bond (of Friendship)], K. 148/125h
   (mm. 4–6 transposed from D to C)

2. Mozart *Die Zufriedenheit im Niedrigen Stande* (Contented with a Humble Lot), K. 151/125f
   (mm. 10–13 transposed from F to C)

3. Mozart *Un moto di Gioja* (A Surge of Joy), K. 579 (mm. 5–8)

4. Mozart *Dans un Bois Solitaire* (In a Lonely Wood), K. 308/295b
   (last 3 mm. transposed from A♭ to C)

5. Mozart *Die Zufriedenheit* (Contentment), K. 349/367a (last phrase transposed from G to C)

6. Mozart *Traurig, doch gelassen* (Sad, Yet Tranquil), K. 391/340b (mm. 7–13 transposed from B♭ to C)

7. Mozart *Gesellenreise (Freimaurerlied)* [Life's Journey (Song of the Freemason)], K. 468
   (mm. 1–2 transposed from B♭ to C)

8. Mozart *Des kleinen Friedrichs Geburtstag* (Little Frederick's Birthday), K. 529
    (last 2 mm. transposed from F to C)

9. Mozart *Zum Schluss* (At the End), K. 484 (last phrase transposed from G to C)

10. Mozart *Die Verschweigung* (Discretion), K. 518 (mm. 10–17 transposed from F to C)

D   Melodies (Major): Chromatic Alterations, Modulating, and Nonmodulating

Section 1. Mozart Songs

The melodies in this part are taken from the Mozart song literature.

Not all of the melodies contain modulations, but in addition to the possibility of modulations, melodies in this part may also include chromatic alterations because of one or another of the following: (1) accompaniments with secondary dominant or leading-tone harmonies; (2) accompaniments with other chromatic harmonies, such as borrowed chords, augmented 6ths, and Neapolitan 6ths; and (3) chromatic nonharmonic tones.

Your instructor will provide directions for the use of syllables or numbers as they relate to the sources of alteration.

Mozart *Das Kinderspiel* (Children's Games), K. 598 (transposed)

1.

Mozart *Warnung* (A Warning), K. 433/416c

3.

Mozart *Gesellenreise (Freimaurerlied)* [Life's Journey (Song of the Freemason)], K. 468

Mozart *Die Zufriedenheit* (Contentment), K. 473

4.

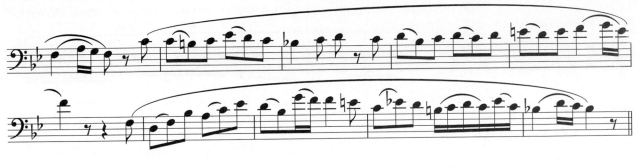

Mozart *Sehnsucht nach dem Frülinge* (Longing for Spring), K. 596 (transposed)

5.

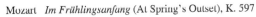

*See unit 13, part B, for d4.

Mozart *Im Frühlingsanfang* (At Spring's Outset), K. 597

6.

Mozart *An Chloe* (To Chloe, 2nd half of song), K. 524 (transposed)

7.

8.

Allegretto moderato

Mozart *Un moto di Gioja* (A Surge of Joy, 2nd half of song), K. 579 (abridged)

9.

No tempo given

Mozart *Die Verschweigung* (Discretion), K. 518

10.

Andante

Mozart *Abendempfindung* (Evening Song, 2nd half of song), K. 523

Section 2. Melodies from Eighteenth-Century Opera by Rameau and Pergolesi

This section includes three melodies from eighteenth-century opera. The first two solo excerpts are sung by Émilie in Rameau's opera-ballet *Les Indes galants* (The Courtly Indies), first performed on August 23, 1735. The third excerpt is sung by Aquilio in Pergolesi's *Adriano in Syria,* which was first performed on October 25, 1734. This area became one of the sources for Stravinsky's *Pulcinella Ballet.* The specific example in the Stravinsky ballet begins at rehearsal 61, "ancora poco meno," ♩ = 86.

Reprinted by arrangement with Broude Brothers Limited.

Reprinted by arrangement with Broude Brothers Limited.

Pergolesi *Adriano in Syria*, Aria: *"Contento forse vivere nel mio martir potrei"* ("Perhaps I Could Live Happily in My Misery") (abridged)

3.

E   Ensembles

The following canons were written by Mozart in 1782 in Vienna. Both are based on texts by Höltv. The first is for two voices (K.V. 230 or K. 382b) and is entitled „Elegie beim Grabe meinen Vaters" ("Elegy at the grave of my father"). The second is for three voices (K.V. 229 or K. 382a) and is entitled „Auf den Tod einer Nachtigall" ("On the death of a Nightingale").

For the convenience of the student and the instructor, two different formats are given. On the left-hand side of the page, the unfamiliar soprano clefs are preserved. On the right-hand side of the page, the same work is presented in the more familiar treble clefs. In the following illustration (ex. A), you will see the opening measures of the first canon written in soprano clef, where the starting note is "c^2" on the top space. In ex. B, you will then see the opening measures written in treble clef, where the starting note is also "c^2" but is written on the second space from the top. Treat these canons as sources for continuous drilling throughout the semester. You might want to begin with the familiar treble clef at first and then come back to the soprano clef when it becomes more familiar. A systematic approach to the soprano clef begins in Unit 13B but you have already encountered an excerpt from Bach's *Art of the Fugue* in the soprano clef in Unit 8D, no. 11.

Mozart   *Selig, selig, alle, alle* [Blessed, Blessed All, All (Who Sleep in the Lord)] Canon for 2 Voices, K. 230

Example A

Mozart   Canon for 2 Voices, K. 230

Example B

Mozart *Selig, selig, alle, alle* [Blessed, Blessed All, All (Who Sleep in the Lord)] Canon for 2 Voices, K. 230

1b.

Mozart *Sie, sie ist dahin* [She Is Gone (The Singer Who Sang the Song of May)] Canon for 3 Voices, K. 229

2b.

Mozart *Terzettino* (Trio): *Soave sia il vento* (May Breezes Blow Lightly), from *Così fan Tutte* (All Women Do the Same), K. 588, no. 10

Andante

Fiordiligi

Dorabella

Don Alfonso

Unit 10

A Rhythm—Simple Meter: Mixed Meters and Irregular Division of the Beat

Section 1. Modules in Simple Meter

Using rhythm syllables or a neutral syllable, sing each of the given modules. Begin by repeating each module several times, then treat the successive modules as a continuous exercise.

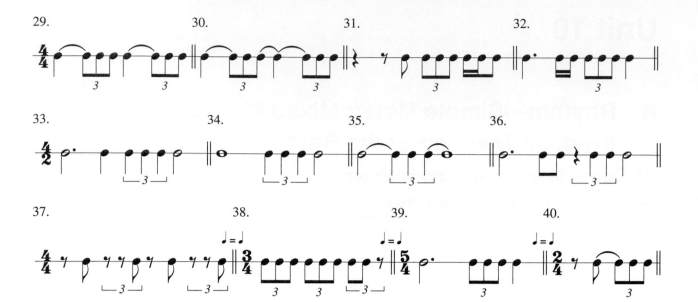

Section 2. Phrases in Simple Meter with Triplets

5.

6. Rhythmic canon

7. Rhythmic ostinato

8. Rhythmic hocket

Section 3. Creating a Coherent Phrase in Simple Meter

Return to section 1 and select three or four rhythm modules. Place them in an order that would create a coherent four-measure phrase.

Write your solution on the following line:

B Diatonic and Chromatic Models and Melodic Fragments for Interval Study—Review: A4 and d5

Section 1. Diatonic and Chromatic Models

As in the previous unit, these exercises focus on the tritone. In this unit, however, the models are based on fragments by a different set of composers: Wagner, Stravinsky, Berg, Franck, Musorgsky, Debussy, Schubert, and Barber. Many of these models are extracted from highly chromatic textures, but the exercises themselves are mostly diatonic. Often the notes of resolution associated with the tritone, in traditional terms, are partially or fully absent in some exercises. **The unifying thread that runs throughout part B of this unit is the pitch-specific nature of the tritone D♯–A.** The one exception occurs in melodic fragments 9–11, where the transposition to relative minor changes D♯–A to F♯–C.

Follow the same procedure as in previous units. Sing the following model in all major keys.

The following table indicates how the models (in this section) relate to the fragments in section 2.

Models	Fragments
1 & 2	1&2
3	3
4	2
5	4
6	6
7	5
8	7
9	8
10	9
11	10
12	11

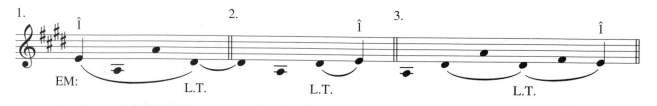

The following model shows how a tritone (A–D♯) is filled in with a M3 (A–C♯) and a M2 (C♯–D♯). The next two models show another way of filling in the same tritone with a M2 (A–B) and a M3 (B–D♯).

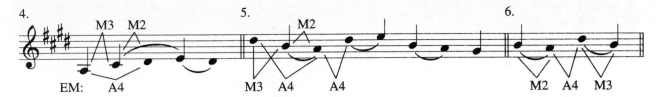

The next three models feature a tritone that is not filled in.

These models relate to fragments 9, 10, and 11 of the next section.

Section 2. Melodic Fragments in E Major (C♯ Minor and E Minor)

1. Wagner *Götterdämmerung* (The Twilight of the Gods), Act III (transposed)

2. Barber "I Hear an Army" (transposed)

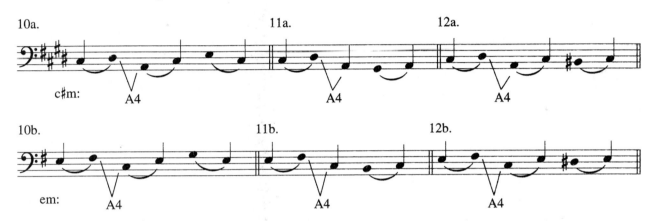

3. Stravinsky *Petroushka,* Third Tableau (transposed)

4. Berg Violin Concerto, I A Carinthian Folk Tune (transposed)

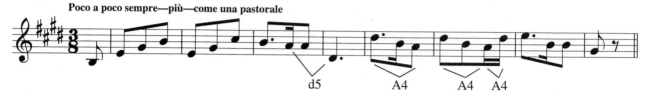

5. Wagner *Götterdämmerung,* Act III, Scene iii

6. Franck Violin Sonata for Violin and Piano (second movement—transposed)

7. Debussy *Des femmes de Paris* (The Dames of Paris), from *Three Ballads of François Villon,* III (transposed)

8. Wagner *Götterdämmerung,* Act III, Scene iii (transposed)

9a. Musorgsky *Boris Godunov,* Act I, Scene i (transposed)

9b.

em:
A4

10a. Schubert *Ihr Bild* (Her Picture) (transposed)

c♯m:
A4

10b.

em:
A4

11a. Barber "Rain Has Fallen" (transposed)

c♯m:
A4

11b.

em:
A4

Section 3. Creating a Coherent Melody

Return to section 2 and select two or three segments of melodic fragments that would create a coherent melody. It may be necessary to change the meter and rhythm of certain segments, depending on your choice.

Section 4. Practice in Clef Reading: Alto Clef and Tenor Clef

Return to the melodic fragments of unit 6 for practice in clef reading. Substitute the alto clef for the treble clef and change the key signature. Return to the melodic fragments of unit 1 for practice in clef reading. Substitute the tenor clef for the treble clef and change the key signature.

C Melodies with Chromatic Alterations

This section contains 12 melodies by the Schumanns. Numbers 1–6 are by Clara Schumann; numbers 7–12 are by Robert Schumann.

The first three melodies are excerpts from Clara Schumann's Three songs, Opus 12 (text by F. Rückert) [attributed to Clara Schumann within Robert Schumann's Liebesfrühling ("Spring of Love", Op. 37, Nos. 2, 4, 11)].

1.

Clara Schumann *Er ist gekommen in Sturm und Regen* (Through Storm and Tempest), op. 12, no. 2 (transposed)

Ruhig

2.

Clara Schumann *Liebst du um Schönheit* (Love You but Beauty), op. 12, no. 4 (transposed)

Bewegter

3.

Clara Schumann *Warum willst du andre fragen?* (Why Inquire of Other People?), op. 12, no. 11 (transposed)

Andante

Here are two other settings by Clara Schumann.

Clara Schumann   *"Ich hab' in deinem Auge"* (I Saw in Your Eye), op. 13, no. 5 (abridged) (text also by Rückert) (transposed)

8.   Robert Schumann   *"Was soll ich sagen"* (What Shall I Say), op. 27, no. 3

                                      Robert Schumann   *"Der Hidalgo"* (The Hidalgo), op. 30, no. 3 (transposed) (abridged)

9.

                                      Robert Schumann   *"Stirb, Lieb' und Freud!"* (Die, Love and Joy), op. 35, no. 2

10.

Robert Schumann   *"Stille Thränen"* (Joy Comes) op. 35, no. 10

11. Sehr langsam

Robert Schumann   *"Nichts Schöneres"* (Nothing More Beautiful), op. 36, no. 3 (transposed) (abridged)

12.   Einfach, innig

D   Melodies with Chromatic Alterations: Modulating

All the melodies in this section are taken from works by Felix Mendelssohn (Songs Without Words). All include alterations due to one or another of the following: (a) accompaniments with secondary-dominant or leading-tone harmonies; (b) accompaniments with other chromatic harmonies such as borrowed chords, augmented 6ths, Neapolitan 6ths, and so on; (c) fully established modulations; and (d) chromatic nonharmonic tones. Your instructor will provide directions for the use of syllables or numbers as they relate to the sources of alteration listed above.

Mendelssohn   Consolation, op. 30, no. 3 (abridged)

Mendelssohn   Venetian Gondola Song, op. 30, no. 6 (abridged) (transposed)

3. **Allegro non troppo**
sehr innig

Mendelssohn The Fleecy Cloud, op. 53, no. 2 (abridged) (transposed)

4. **Adagio cantabile**

Mendelssohn Sadness of Soul, op. 53, no. 4 (abridged)

5. **Andante espressivo**

Mendelssohn May Breezes, op. 62, no. 1 (abridged) (transposed)

6. **Allegretto grazioso**

Mendelssohn Spring Song, op. 62, no. 6 (adapted and abridged)

7. **Andante sostenuto**

Mendelssohn Elegy, op. 85, no. 4 (abridged) (transposed)

Mendelssohn Retrospection, op. 102, no. 2 (abridged) (transposed)

Mendelssohn *Tarantella,* op. 102, no. 3 (abridged) (transposed)

Mendelssohn Belief, op. 102, no. 6 (abridged)

E   Ensembles

1.

Beethoven *Freundschaft* (Friendship), Canon for Three Voices, WoO 164

2.

G.P. Telemann *Fuga 2* (Fugue)

Unit 11

A Rhythm—Compound Meter and Simple Meter: Irregular Divisions of the Beat (the Quartolet in Compound Meter, and the Triplet in Simple Meter)

Section 1. Modules in Compound Meter and Simple Meter

Begin by repeating each module several times. Then treat the successive modules as a continuous exercise. Modules in compound meter are in measures 1–40; those for simple meter are in measures 41–48.

Rhythm Syllables

Use the following syllables for the quartolet if your instructor recommends you do so.

Section 2. Phrases in Compound Meter and Simple Meter with Irregular Divisions of the Beat

3.

4.

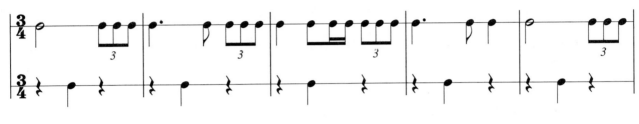

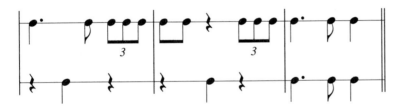

5. Rhythmic ostinato

6. Upper rhythm repeated twice in lower voice in diminution

Section 3. Creating Coherent Phrases in Compound Meter and Simple Meter

Return to section 1 and select three or four rhythm modules, first in compound meter and then in simple meter. Place the modules in two coherent four-measure phrases, one in compound meter and the other in simple meter.

Write your solutions on the following lines:

Compound meter:

_____||

Simple meter:

_____||

B Diatonic and Chromatic Models and Melodic Fragments for Interval Study— New Intervals: d7 and A2

Section 1. Diatonic and Chromatic Models

The models in this section emphasize intervals of the diminished 7th (d7) and the augmented 2nd (A2).

The exercises in this section are in G♯ minor and relate to the music of Bach, Haydn, Beethoven, and Wagner. The models in this section relate to the fragments in the next section as follows:

Models	Fragments
1	1
2	2
3	3, 4, 5, 6
4	5
5	7a,b,c,d
6	7a,b,c,d
7	7a,b,c,d
8a	8
8b	8
9	11, 12, 13, 14
10	11, 12, 13, 14, 15

Models 1–4

All the d7s in these models extend from F**x** up to E or from E down to F**x**.

Follow the same procedures as found in previous units. For extra practice, sing the first model in all minor keys, transposing to each new key by P5s down or P4s up (see model below). Because the d7 is so neatly framed by the tonic triad, these patterns are excellent for "tossing," as in previous units.

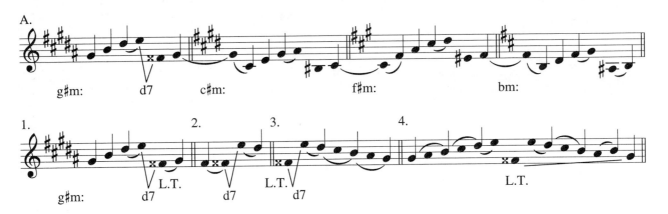

Models 5–7

Models 5–7 outline the basic motives of the opening notes of Beethoven's Quartet, op. 133 (The Grand Fugue). Melodic fragments 7a, b, c, and d are from the same quartet. Memorize model 7 so you can "hear" these fragments with your eyes when you reach section 2.

Models 8a and 8b

These models focus on the A2 (from F**x** down to E or from E up to F**x**) representing the inversion of the d7. These A2s have the same pitches as the d7s in models 1–4. The leading-tone 7th chord in first inversion (vii°$^6_5$) is indicated in 8b and emphasizes the symmetry of the d7 chord.

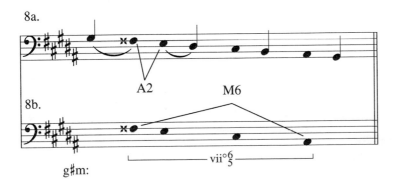

Models 9–10

The leading-tone 7th chord, in root position, outlines the d7 chord and emphasizes the resulting symmetry (m3s or their enharmonic equivalent).

g#m: d7   d7   d7   d7

Section 2. Melodic Fragments in G♯ Minor

1. Bach *Musikalisches Opfer* (The Musical Offering) (transposed)

d7

2. Beethoven String Quartet, op. 132, I

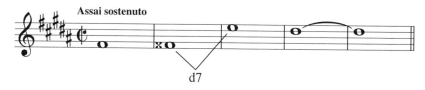

d7

3. Beethoven String Quartet, op. 133, I (transposed)

d7

4. Bach Two-Part Invention, no. 4 (transposed)

d7 d7

5. Bach Three-Part Invention, no. 2 (transposed)

d7 d7

6. Bach Two-Part Invention, no. 2 (transposed)

d7

7a. Beethoven String Quartet, op. 133, First Section (transposed)

d7   d7

7b. Beethoven String Quartet, op. 133, First Section (transposed)

d7   d7

7c. Beethoven String Quartet, op. 133, First Section (transposed)

d7   d7

7d. Beethoven String Quartet, op. 133, First Section (transposed)

d7   d7

8. Haydn Piano Sonata XVI: 16 (transposed)

A2

9. Haydn Piano Sonata XVI: 12 II (transposed)

A2

10. Haydn Song *Dir nah ich mich, nah mich dem Throne* (I Approach You, I Approach the Throne) (transposed)

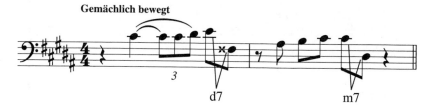

11. Wagner *Götterdämmerung,* Act III, Scene ii (transposed)

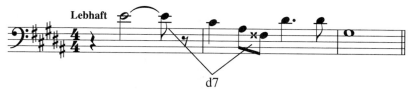

12. Wagner *Götterdämmerung,* Act III, Scene i (transposed)

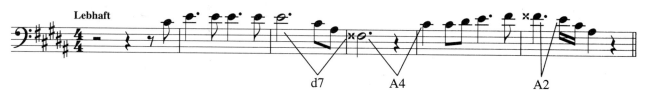

13. Wagner *Götterdämmerung,* Act III, Scene i (transposed)

14. Wagner *Götterdämmerung,* Prelude (adapted and transposed)

15. Bach *Well-Tempered Clavier,* Book I, Fugue 24 (transposed)

Section 3. Creating a Coherent Melody

Return to section 2 and select two or three segments of melodic fragments that would create a coherent melody. It may be necessary to change the meter and rhythm of certain segments depending on your choice.

Section 4. Practice in Clef Reading: Alto Clef and Tenor Clef

Return to the melodic fragments of unit 7 for practice in clef reading. Substitute the alto clef for the treble clef and change the key signature. Return to the melodic fragments of unit 3 for practice in clef reading. Substitute the tenor clef for the treble clef and change the key signature.

C   Melodies with Unusual Modal Characteristics

These melodies are from various countries, including Russia, Ireland, Ethiopia, the former Czechoslovakia, and France. Some of these melodies are taken directly from the folk song literature. Others represent settings by composers such as Igor Stravinsky and Samuel Barber. The Stravinsky settings were written in Morges, Switzerland. C. F. Ramuz translated the Russian words into French. The song by Samuel Barber is based on a poem in French by Rainer Maria Rilke. Although the texts of these songs are not given in this unit, you are encouraged to seek out the modern settings of these works by studying scores in your library.

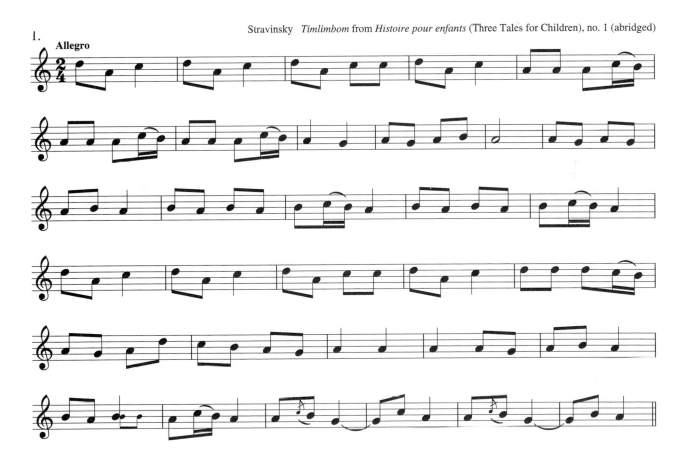

Stravinsky *Timlimbom* from *Histoire pour enfants* (Three Tales for Children), no. 1 (abridged)

2.

From *Songs of the Irish* by Donal O'Sullivan, published by the Mercier Press, 4 Bridge Street, Cork, Ireland. Reprinted by permission.

3.

"Derreen Day" from *Songs of the Irish*

From *Songs of the Irish* by Donal O'Sullivan, published by the Mercier Press, 4 Bridge Street, Cork, Ireland. Reprinted by permission.

Chant des chrétiens d'éthiopie (Song of the Christians of Ethiopia) from *Chansons nègres* (Black Songs), vol. II, collected by Julien Tiersot

Largement et librement

4. *Se conformer aux valeurs, sans s'astreindre à une mesure régulière.*

5.

Květ Broskví (Fleur du Pecher)—1932 by Bohuslav Martinů, Rev. Jan Hanus. Published 1980, Praha, *Bärenreiter-Verlag*—Kassell and Basel

Samuel Barber *Le clocher chante* (The Bell Tower Sings), from *Mélodies passàgeres* (Transitory Melodies), op. 27, no. 4

6.

7. Stravinsky *Chanson pour compter* (Counting Song), from *Quatre Chants Russes* (Four Russian Songs), no. 2 (abridged)

8. Stravinsky *Canarde* (The Drake) *Ronde* from *Quatre Chants Russes* (Four Russian Songs), no. 1 (abridged)

Canard (Ronde) by Igor Stravinsky. Masters Music Publications, Inc., P.O. Box 810157, Boca Raton, Florida 33481-0157. Published in U.S.

9.

Poco pesante

"Farewell to Carraig An Éide" from *Songs of the Irish*. Published by Mercier Press, Cork, Ireland.

10.

"'Tis the last rose of summer"   Air: *Groves of Blarney,* from Holden (modified by Moore)

D   Melodies—Chromatic Alterations:
Modulating and Nonmodulating

Section 1. Sacred Melodies from Various Sources

All these melodies are sacred and include works by Ellington and Berlioz as well as a Negro spiritual (Deep River) and two examples of Gregorian Chant (Hymn to St. Thomas Aquinas, *In Paradisum,* from the Requiem Mass). The last four examples are from the *Complete Collection of Irish Music* by George Petrie (1789–1866), edited by Charles Villiers Stanford (1902): The Hymn of St. Bernard, The Funeral Cry (Galway, 1840), a Christmas Hymn (Galway), and an Irish Hymn (Londonderry).

1.

Duke Ellington   "David Danced" (Sacred Concert no. 1)

Brightly

Duke Ellington "David Danced" from *First Sacred Concert* by Duke Ellington. Copyright © 1963 (Renewed) by G. Schirmer, Inc. (ASCAP) International Copyright Secured. All Rights Reserved. Reprinted by Permission.

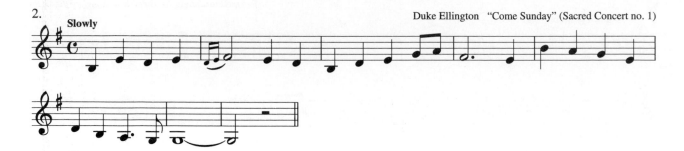

2.

Slowly

Duke Ellington "Come Sunday" (Sacred Concert no. 1)

Duke Ellington "Come Sunday" (Sacred Concert no. 1). Copyright © 1946 (Renewed) by G. Schirmer, Inc. (ASCAP) International. Copyright Secured. All rights reserved. Reprinted by permission.

3.

"Deep River"   Negro Spiritual

Adagio

4.

Berlioz   *Dignare Domine* (Prayer), *Te Deum*

Moderato quasi andantino

5.

Hymn to St. Thomas Aquinas   Gregorian Chant

6.

In Paradisum (Into Paradise)   Gregorian Chant

7.

Jesu dulcis memoria (The Hymn of St. Bernard)   from Mr. Southwell

8.

Agitato

Funeral Cry Galway, August 28th, 1840

9.

Lento (♩ = 69)

Christmas Carol or Hymn (as sung in the county of Galway)   from Mrs. Close

10.

Andante

Irish Hymn Sung on the Dedication of a Chapel, Co. of Londonderry

Section 2. Songs by Brahms

All the following melodies are excerpts from songs by Brahms.

1. **Sehr lebhaft**

Brahms *Tambourliedchen* (The Little Drummer's Song), op. 69, no. 5 (abridged and transposed)

2. **Etwas bewegt**

Brahms *Therese*, op. 86, no. 1 (abridged)

3. **Bewegt und heimlich**

Brahms *Spannung* (Tension), op. 84, no. 5 (abridged and transposed)

4. **Andante moderato**

Brahms *Anklänge* (Reminiscences), op. 7, no. 3 (abridged)

E Ensembles

1.

Bach *Sei gegrüsset, Jesu gütig* (Hail to Thee, Jesus Kind), from Var. X, BWV 768

outer voices

* original is an octavo lower

2.

Schubert Fantasy for Piano and Violin, op. 159

The B♭ clarinet sounds a M2 lower than written. Use the tenor clef to indicate c'' in singing the transposition. Check your accuracy in the reading of the clarinet part with the harp part. Both lines sound in unison.

Mahler *Der Abschied* (The Farewell), from *Das Lied von der Erde* (Song of the Earth)

Die Blu - men blass - en im Däm - mer - schein.

Unit 12

A Rhythm—Compound Meter and Simple Meter: Subdivisions of the Beat into Eight Parts

Section 1. Modules in Compound Meter and Simple Meter

Begin by repeating each module several times. Then treat the successive modules as a continuous exercise.

Rhythm Syllables

Use the following syllables for the eight note subdivisions if your instructor recommends you do so.

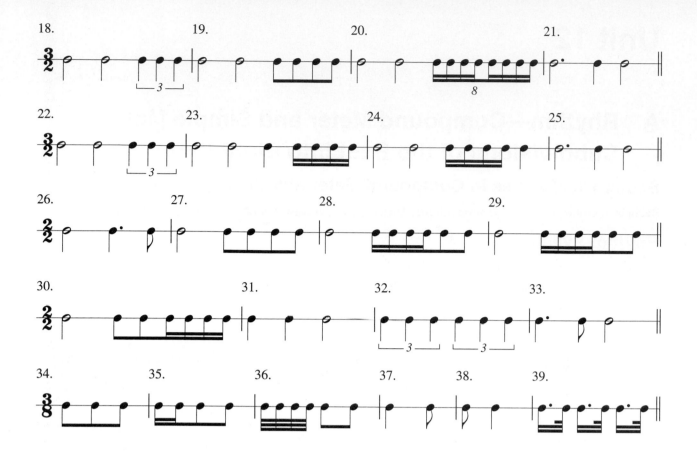

Section 2. Phrases in Compound Meter and Simple Meter with Subdivisions of the Beat into Eight Parts

3.

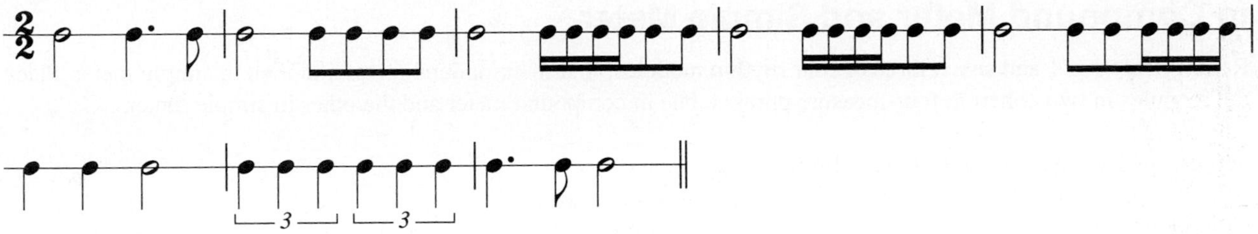

4.

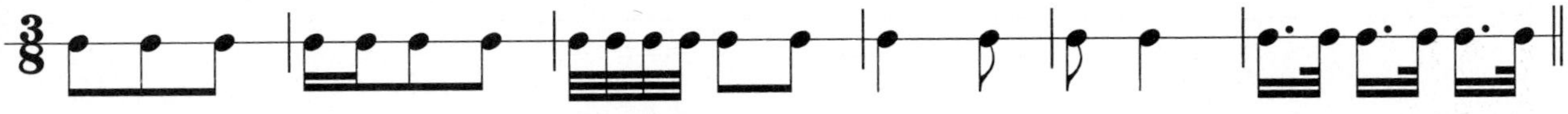

5.

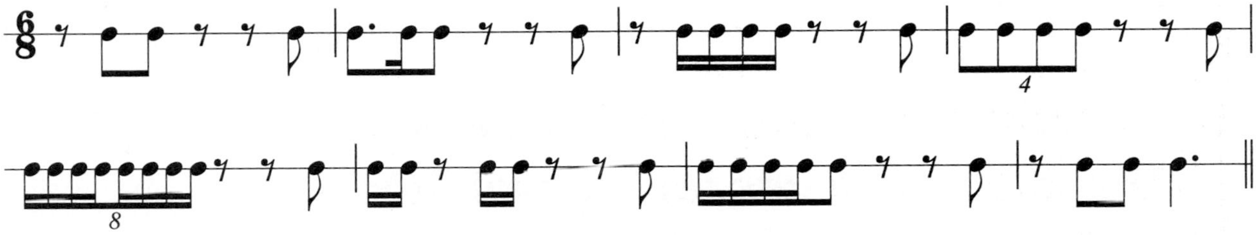

6.

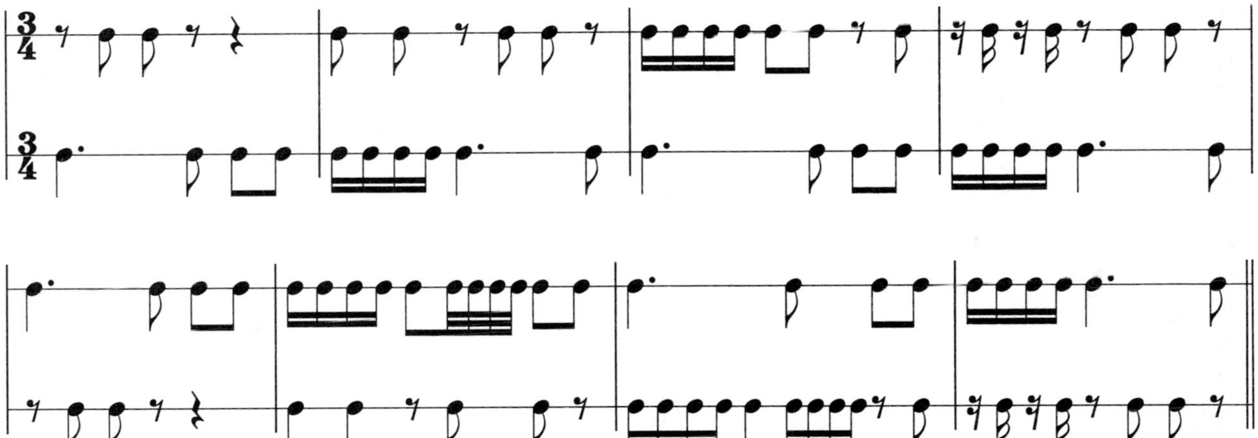

Section 3. Creating Coherent Phrases in Compound Meter and Simple Meter

Return to section 1 and select three or four rhythm modules, first in compound meter and then in simple meter. Place the modules in two coherent four-measure phrases, one in compound meter and the other in simple meter.

Write your solutions on the following lines:

Compound meter:

_____ ‖

Simple meter:

_____ ‖

B Diatonic and Chromatic Models and Melodic Fragments for Interval Study— New Intervals: A6 and d3

Section 1. Diatonic and Chromatic Models

The models in this section emphasize intervals of the augmented 6th (A6) and the diminished 3rd (d3).

The exercises in this section are in B minor or B major and relate to the music of Beethoven and Mozart. When you reach the next section, you will notice that a bass line is provided for most of the fragments to show voice-leading principles involving the augmented 6th (A6) and its resolution to an octave (on the dominant). Implied harmonies are also provided.

The models in this section relate to the fragments of the next section as follows:

Models	Fragments
1, 2, 3, 4	1, 2, 3, 4
5, 6	5, 6*
7, 8, 9	8, 9, 10

* The model for fragment 7 appears as 7a in Section 2.

Exercises 1–4

These models follow the contour of the A6 chord, outlining each factor.

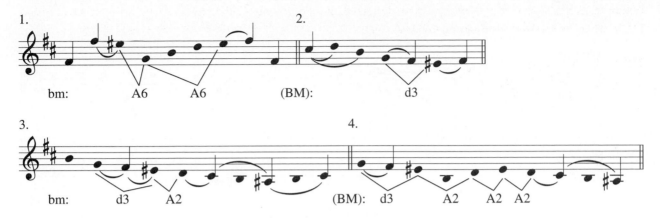

Exercises 5–6

If the implications of A6 chords are not apparent in these exercises, they will become more evident in the melodic fragments (section D), where a second voice is added.

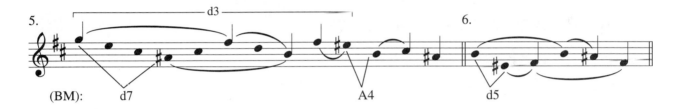

Exercises 7–9

These exercises show how the A6 chord might be used as a pivot chord in modulations. For additional practice, repeat these patterns in various different keys in an attempt to out-modulate both Beethoven and Mozart.

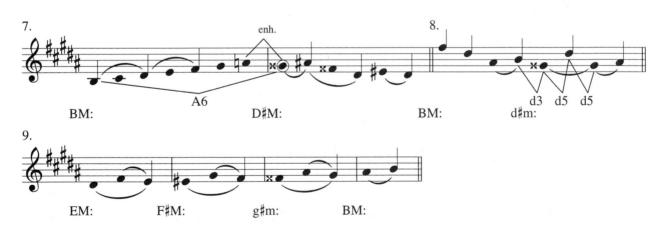

Section 2. Melodic Fragments in B Minor and B Major

Melodic Fragments for Interval Study—New Intervals: A6 and d3

1. Beethoven   Theme, WoO 80 (transposed) (abridged)

2. Mozart   *La finta giardiniera* (Opera) (The Girl in Gardener's Disguise) (transposed)

3. Mozart   Recitative from *Les noces de Figaro* (The Marriage of Figaro) (Opera)

4. Mozart   *La Clemenza di Tito* (Opera) (Titus's Clemency) (transposed) (abridged)

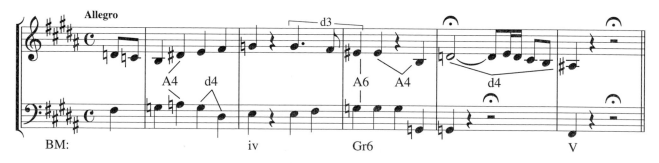

5. Mozart *La Clemenza di Tito* (Opera) (Titus's Clemency) (transposed) (abridged)

BM: iv   I   iv   V   i   Fr6   V

6. Mozart *Les noces de Figaro* (The Marriage of Figaro) (Opera) (transposed)

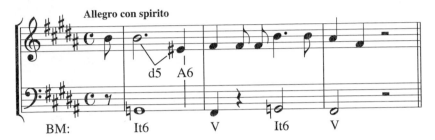

BM: It6   V   It6   V

7. Mozart *Les noces de Figaro* (The Marriage of Figaro) (Opera) (transposed)

BM: [V$_2^4$]*   IV^6 [V$_2^4$]   IV^6 It6   V   It6   V

* Secondary dominant

7a. Reduction of no. 7

8. Beethoven Symphony no. V, op. 67, II (transposed)

EM: V
or
BM: I   V7
                 V7 of IV   D#M: Gr6*   or {I$_4^6$ V^7
                                      or   V$_6^8$ ———— 7   I
                                      Gr$_3^4$ $_4^5$ ———— $_3^5$

* Functions as doubly A4

9. Mozart *La finta giardiniera* (Opera) (The Girl in Gardener's Disguise) (transposed)

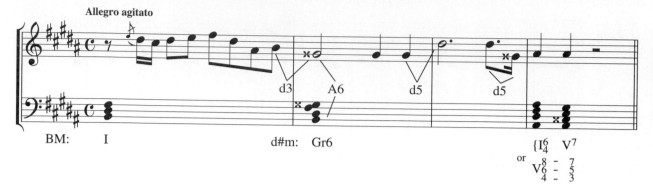

10. Mozart *Die Entführung aus dem Serail* (Opera) (The Abduction from the Seraglio) (transposed)

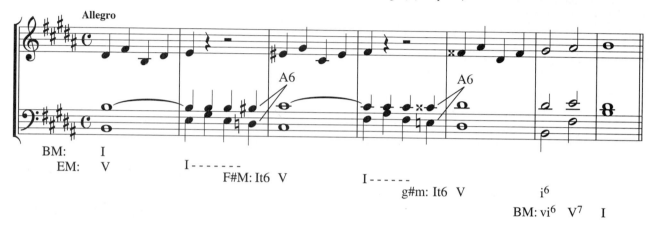

Supplemental fragments to show voice-leading principles involving the diminished third (G♮–E♯) brought about by the motion of the lowered second scale degree (G♮) to the leading tone (E♯) and tonic (F♯).

Beethoven   Variations on "God Save the King," WoO 78 (Var. 5, m. 5—transposed from C minor)

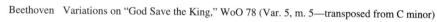

Purcell   King Arthur (Frost Scene)—Frost Genius (transposed from C minor)

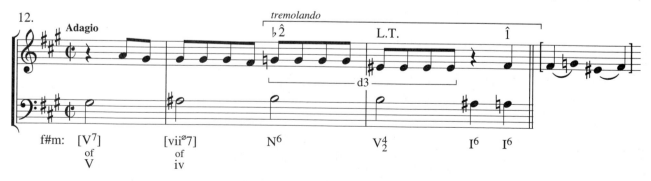

Section 3. Creating a Coherent Melody

Return to section 2 and select two or three segments of melodic fragments that would create a coherent melody. It may be necessary to change the meter and rhythm of certain segments, depending on your choice.

Section 4. Practice in Clef Reading: Alto Clef and Tenor Clef

Return to the melodic fragments of unit 8 for practice in clef reading. Substitute the alto clef for the treble clef and change the key signature. Return to the melodic fragments of unit 4 for practice in clef reading. Substitute the tenor clef for the treble clef and change the key signature.

C   Melodies with Unusual Modal Characteristics

As with the melodies in unit 11, part C, some of these melodies are from various countries, including Bulgaria, Greece, Ireland, Israel, Russia, Spain, and the United States. Others represent settings by composers such as Musorgsky and Prokofiev. These 20 songs illustrate melodic patterns that are characteristic of modes such as dorian, phrygian, lydian, mixolydian, and aeolian and combinations one or more of these modes.

Dies Irae (Day of Wrath) Gregorian chant (*Mass for the Dead*) Dorian mode

1.

Dies Irae (Day of Wrath)—as sung in the Co. of Londonderry

2.

3.

Allegretto

Ireland "A Bold Child" (Ionian mode)

Chorus

From *Songs of the Irish* by Donal O'Sullivan, published by the Mercier Press, 4, Bridge Street, Cork, Ireland.

4.

Sharp/Karpeles "Barbara Ellen" (Pentatonic)

Allegro

Sharp/Karpeles. "Barbara Ellen" from *80 Appalachian Folk Songs.* © Copyright 1968 by Faber Music, Ltd. London. Copyright Renewed. Reprinted by permission of Boosey & Hawkes, Inc., U.S. & Canadian Agent.

5.

Folk song Greece (Dorian mode)

Folk song "Eliza" (Dorian/aeolian modes)

6.

Lento

"Eliza" published by Blackstaff Press, Belfast, Northern Ireland. Used by permission of the Estate of Sam Henry.

7.

"Berceuse (Aeolian Mode)" from *Expositions and Developments* by Igor Stravinsky and Robert Craft. Copyright © 1959, 1960, 1961, 1962, Igor Stravinsky. Reprinted by permission of the Regents of the University of California Press, Berkeley, California.

Y. Ezrachi, Arr. by A. W. Binder *Yesh Banu Ko-ach* (Our Strength within Us) (Aeolian mode)

8.

Yesh Banu Ko-ach (Our Strength Within Us) English Lyric by Y. Ezrachi. Arranged by A.W. Binder. Copyright © 1942 by Edward B. Marks Music Company. Copyright Renewed. International Copyright Secured. All Rights Reserved. Used by Permission.

9. **Allegro vigoroso** (♩=120)

Artsah Alinu (Come to the Land) Israel (Aeolian mode)

Artsah Alinu (Come to the Land). English Lyric by Olga Paul. Arranged by A.W. Binder. Copyright © 1942 by Edward B. Marks Music Company. Copyright Renewed. International Copyright Secured. All Rights Reserved. Used by permission.

10.

"The Lone Rock" (Folk song) Ireland (Aeolian mode)

From *Songs of the Irish* by Donal O'Sullivan, published by the Mercier Press, 4, Bridge Street, Cork, Ireland.

11.

"Young Lad" (Folk song) Ireland (Ionian mode)

From *Songs of the Irish* by Donal O'Sullivan, published by the Mercier Press, 4, Bridge Street, Cork, Ireland.

Russian folk song   "My Sweetheart" (Aeolian/phrygian modes)

12.

Musorgsky   *Boris Godunov,* "Polonaise" (Lydian mode)

Alla polacca
13. **Non troppo allegro**

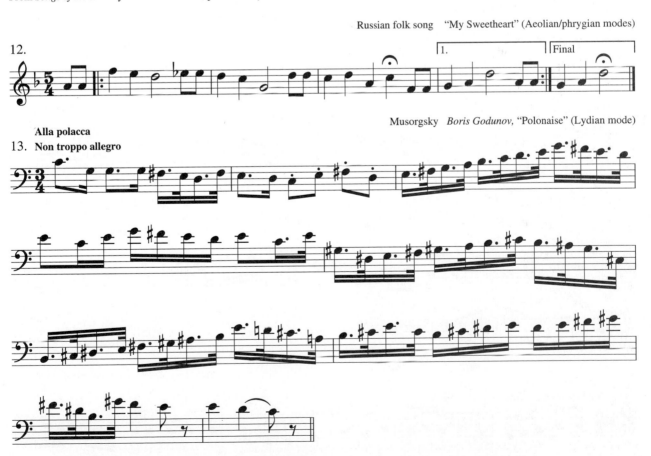

14.

Irish folk song "The Fair Hills of E'ire O!" (Mixolydian mode)

From *Songs of the Irish* by Donald O'Sullivan, published by the Mercier Press, 4, Bridge Street, Cork, Ireland.

15.

Irish folk song "The Soft Deal Board" (Mixolydian mode)

From *Songs of the Irish* by Donald O'Sullivan, published by the Mercier Press, 4, Bridge Street, Cork, Ireland.

16.

Bulgarian folk song (Modal mixture)

Prokofiev *Katerina*, op. 104, no. 4 (abridged)

17. **Moderato scherzando**

Charles Wakefield Cadman   "He Who Moves in the Dew"*

18.   Allegretto con semplicità

* A Chippewa Indian theme collected by Frances Densmore

Spanish   *Navalafuente*

19.   Villancico   ♩ = 116

"Villancico" Matos, Pares & Figueras.

Irish folk song   "The Blackthorn Tree"

20.   Affettuoso

D Melodies—Chromatic Alterations: Modulating and Nonmodulating

Section 1. Melodies by Schubert

All the melodies in this section contain modulations.

1. **Langsam**

Schubert *Wasserflut* (Flood of Tears), from *Winterreise* (Winter Journey), D. 911, no. 6

2. **Nicht zu geschwind**

Schubert *Rückblick* (Glance Back), from *Winterreise*, D. 911, no. 8

3. **Mässig**

Schubert *Rast* (Rest), from *Winterreise*, D. 911, no. 10

Schubert *Einsamkeit* (Solitude), from *Winterreise,* D. 911, no. 12

Schubert *Die Post* (The Mail Coach), from *Winterreise,* D. 911, no. 13

Schubert *Im Dorfe* (In the Village), from *Winterreise,* D. 911, no. 17

6.

Schubert *Der Stürmische* (The Stormy Morning), from *Winterreise,* D. 911, no. 18

7. **Ziemlich geschwind, doch dräftig**

Schubert *Täuschung* (Deception), from *Winterreise,* D. 911, no. 19

8. **Etwas geschwind**

9.

Schubert *Das Wirtshaus* (The Inn), from *Winterreise,* D. 911, no. 21

Sehr langsam

10. **Ziemlich geschwind**

Section 2. Clef Reading and Transposition

Melodies in this section are from songs by Gustav Mahler, his wife Alma, and Fanny Mendelssohn Hensel (sister of Felix Mendelssohn).

Transpose this melody down a m3 by thinking in soprano clef. Substitute the A major key signature. The starting note is a (the a' above middle C).

Gustav Mahler *Das Trinklied vom Jammer der Erde* (The Drinking Song of the Earth's Lament), from *Das Lied von der Erde* (The Song of the Earth)

1. **Allegro pesante with vigor**

Transpose this melody down a m3 by thinking in soprano clef. Substitute the D major key signature for lines 1 and 2 and G major for lines 3 and 4. The starting note for each excerpt is:

Excerpt W: d" (octave and a 2nd above middle C)
Excerpt X: g' (above middle C)
Excerpt Y: c" (above middle C)

Gustav Mahler *Der Einsame im Herbst* (The Lonely One in Autumn), from *Das Lied von der Erde*

2. **Sostenuto**

3.

* The clarinet is in B♭. Transpose down a M2 by thinking in tenor clef. Substitute the B♭ major key signature.
The starting note is b♭' (above middle C, c').

Transpose down a m3 by thinking in soprano clef. Substitute the key signature for G. The starting note is d.'

4.

Gustav Mahler *Von der Jugend* (Of Youth), from *Das Lied von der Erde*

Gustav Mahler *Nun will die Sonn' so hell aufgehn!* (Now the Sun Will Rise So Brightly),
from *Kinder-Totenlieder* (Songs on the Death of Children), no. 1

5.

6.

Gustav Mahler *Der Tamboursg'sell* (The Drummer Boy)

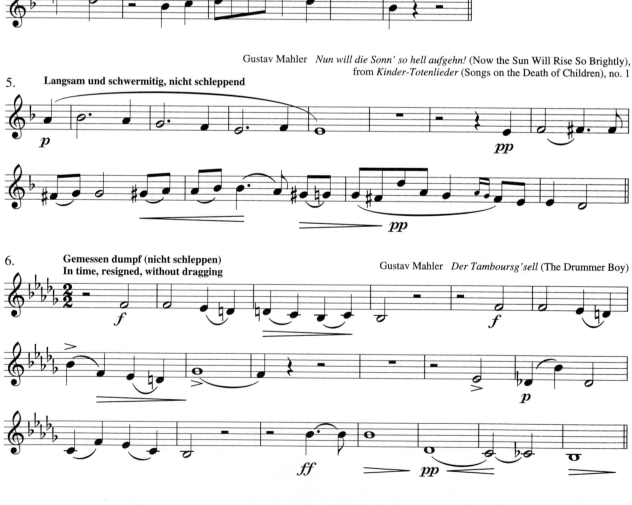

Gustav Mahler *Wenn mein Schatz Hochzeit* (My Sweetheart's Wedding Day),
from *Lieder eines fahrenden Gesellen* (Songs of a Wayfarer), no. 1

7.

Gustav Mahler *Ging heut' Morgen über's Feld* (This Morning I Went through the Fields), from *Lieder eines fahrenden Gesellen,* no. 2

8.

Alma Mahler *Der Erkennende* (The Realization)

9.

10.   Fanny Mendelssohn Hensel *Schwanenlied* (Swansong)

E. Ensembles

Brahms *Ich weiss* (I Wonder Why the Dove So Sad Is Cooing!), from *Thirteen Canons,* op. 113, no. 11;   text by Rückert

1.

Ich weiss nicht was im Hain die Taub - be __ gir - ret!

Ob sie be - trübt wie mei - ne See - le har - ret des

Freun - des, der __ von __ ihr sich hat ver - ir - ret? Des

Freun-des, der von ihr __ sich _ hat __ ver - ir - ret?

2.

Schütz *Introitus* (Introit), from *Die sieben Worte Jesu Christi* (The Seven Last Words of Christ)

Cantus

Altus

Tenor I

Tenor II

Bassus

Continuus

Da Je - sus an ___ dem Kreu - ze

Da Je - sus an - dem Kreu - ze ___

Da Je - sus an dem Kreu - ze

Da Je - sus ___ an dem Kreu - ze

stund da Je - sus

stund und ihm sein Leich - nam war ___ ver - wund't, du Je -

stund und ihm sein Leich-nam war ver - wund't,

stund und ihm sein Leich-nam war ___ ver - wund't, du Je -

Da Je -

Unit 13

A Rhythm—Simple Meter: The Supertriplet

Section 1. Modules in Simple Meter

Begin by repeating each module several times. Then treat the successive modules as a continuous exercise.

Rhythm Syllables

Use the following syllables for the supertriplet if your instructor recommends you do so.

Section 2. Phrases in Simple Meter with Supertriplets

Section 3. Creating a Coherent Phrase in Simple Meter with Supertriplets

Return to section 1 and select three or four rhythm modules. Place the modules into a coherent four-measure phrase.

Write your solution on the following line:

B Diatonic and Chromatic Models and Melodic Fragments for Interval Study—New Interval: d4

Section 1. Diatonic and Chromatic Models

The models in this section emphasize the diminished 4th (d4) and relate to the music of Ellington, Liszt, Bach, Beethoven, Haydn, and Schubert (see section 2). The models (exercises) of this section prefigure the fragments in the following manner:

Models	Fragments
1, 2	1, 2
3, 4	3, 4
5	5, 6, 7
6	5, 8
7	10
8	8, 10

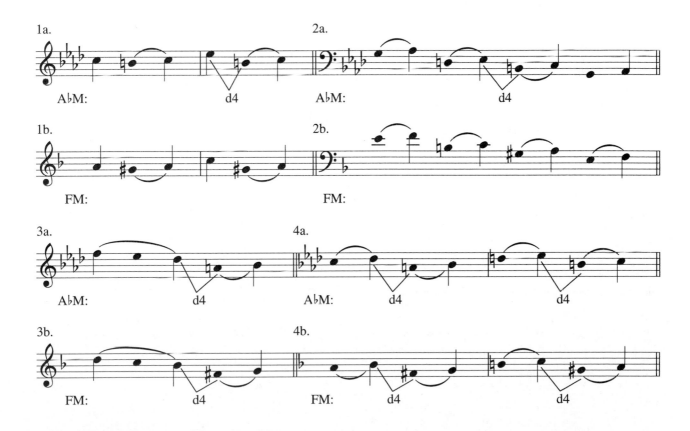

For further practice, sing exercise 5 in all minor keys, transposing to each new key by P5s down or P4s up. (see model below)

fm: b♭ m: e♭ m:

L.T.

fm:

Section 2. Melodic Fragments in A♭ Major
(F Major and F Minor)

A♭ major:

1a.   Ellington "Mood Indigo"

d4

"Mood Indigo" by Duke Ellington, Irving Mills, and Albany Bigard. © 1931 (Renewed), Assigned to EMI Mills Music, Inc., Famous Music Corporation and Indigo Mood Music in USA. All Rights outside USA controlled by EMI Mills Music, Inc. All Rights Reserved. Used by permission of WARNER BROS. PUBLICATIONS U.S. Inc., Miami, FL 33014, Famous Music Corporation and Indigo Mood Music.

2a.   Haydn String Quartet, op. 76, no. 4, I (transposed) (adapted)

d5   d4

3a.   Haydn *Das strickende Mädchen* (The Knitting Girl) (transposed)

d4

4a.   Liszt *Freudvoll und leidvoll* (Full of Joy and Full of Sorrow)

d4   d4

F major:

1b. Ellington "Mood Indigo"

2b. Haydn   String Quartet, op. 76, no. 4, I

3b. Haydn   *Das strickende Mädchen* (The Knitting Girl) (transposed)

F Minor:

5. Schubert   *Der Doppelgänger* (The Wraith) (transposed)

6. Bach   Fugue no. IV from *Well-Tempered Clavier,* Book I (transposed)

7. Schubert   *Am Meer* (By the Sea) (transposed)

8. Schubert   *Der Atlas* (The Atlas) (transposed)

9. Haydn Piano Sonata XVI:5, Trio (transposed)

10. Beethoven Piano Sonata, op. 111, I (transposed)

11. Hadyn String Quartet, op. 74, no. 3, I (transposed) (adapted)

12. Liszt *Die Vätergruft* (The Ancestral Vault)

13. Liszt *Die Vätergruft* (The Ancestral Vault)

Section 3. Creating a Coherent Melody

Return to section 2 and select two or three segments of melodic fragments that would create a coherent melody. It may be necessary to change the meter and rhythm of certain segments, depending on your choice.

Section 4. Practice in Clef Reading: Alto, Tenor, and Soprano Clefs

Return to the melodic fragments of unit 9 for practice in clef reading. Substitute the alto clef for the treble clef and change the key signature. Return to the melodic fragments of unit 5 for practice in clef reading. Substitute the tenor clef for the treble clef and change the key signature. Return to the melodic fragments of unit 1 for practice in clef reading. Substitute the soprano clef for the treble clef and change the key signature.

C Melodies from the Blues Repertoire

The first eight melodies are by composers such as Chris Smith, Perry Bradford, Cab Calloway, and Count Basie. Melody 9 ("Island in the Sun") is by Harry Belafonte and Lord Burgess. The last melody in this section ("New York, New York") is the theme from the motion picture by the same name.

Chris Smith "Ballin' the Jack"

1. Moderato

Chris Smith Boom, Tum, Ta-Ra-Ra—Zing Boom! Lyrics by Ferd. E. Mierisch

2. Moderato

Boom, tum-ta-ra-ra   Zing Boom!

Boom, tum-ta-ra-ra   Zing Boom!

Boom, Tum, Ta-Ra - Ra   -   Zing Boom!

Boom tum-ta - ra   -   ra! Zing   Boom! Zing

3.

Perry Bradford   That Thing Called Love

Moderato

Perry Bradford Crazy Blues

5. **Moderato**

Words by Mitch Parish, Music by Frank Perkins and Cab Calloway "The Skat Song"

Chorus

skat' n   skeet' n

hi - de hi - and skat-tle at - tle at da day ___

skat' n   skeet' n   hi - de hi, ___ and skat-tle at - tle at da day ___

___

skat' n   skeet' n   hi - de hi, ___ and skat-tle at - tle at da day ___

"The Scat Song" Music by Frank Perkins, Cab Calloway, Words by Mitchell Parish. Reprinted by permission of Mills Music.

6.

Count Basie "King Joe (Joe Louis Blues)" (abridged)

Slow blues tempo

"King Joe (Joe Louis Blues)." Music by Count Basie. Copyright © 1942. Bregman, Vocco & Conn.

7.

James Rushing, Count Basie, and Ed Durham "Good Morning Blues"

Count Basie, Jerry Livingston, and Mack David "Blue and Sentimental"

8.

9. **Slowly—freely**   Harry Belafonte and Lord Burgess   "Island in the Sun"

10. **Moderately, with rhythm**   F. Ebb, J. Kander   Theme from *New York, New York*

D Melodies by Duke Ellington

Chord changes for the Ellington melodies are given to inspire your keyboard harmonizations. Whenever possible, harmonize the melodies and accompany them as you sing.

Billy Strayhorn and the Delta Rhythm Boys "Take the 'A' Train"

1. **Rhythmically**

Duke Ellington, Irving Mills, and Rex Stewart "Boy Meets Horn"

2. **Moderato**

Duke Ellington, Eddie DeLange, and Irving Mills "Solitude"

3. **Slowly, with expression**

4. **Slowly**

"Mood Indigo" by Duke Ellington, Irving Mills, and Albany Bigard. © 1931 (Renewed), Assigned to EMI Mills Music, Inc., Famous Music Corporation and Indigo Mood Music in the USA. All Rights outside USA controlled by EMI Mills Music, Inc. All Rights Reserved. Used by Permission of WARNER BROS. PUBLICATIONS U.S. INC., Miami, FL 33014, Famous Music Corporation and Indigo Mood Music.

Duke Ellington, Irving Mills, and Manny Kurtz   "In a Sentimental Mood"

5. **Slowly with expression**

"In a Sentimental Mood" by Duke Ellington, Irving Mills, and Manny Kurtz. © 1935 (Renewed) EMI Mills Music, Inc. and Famous Music Corporation in USA. All Rights outside USA controlled by EMI Mills Music, Inc. All Rights Reserved. Used by Permission of WARNER BROS. PUBLICATIONS U.S. INC., Miami FL 33014 and Famous Music Corporation.

Duke Ellington and Billy Strayhorn   "Day Dream"

6.

Slow

Duke Ellington, Harry James, and Don George   "Everything but You"

7.   **Moderate and rhythmic**

Duke Ellington and Paul Webster   "I Got it Bad"(And That Ain't Good)
from the American Revuc Theatre Production *Jump for Joy*

8.   **Moderately**

9. **Slowly**   Duke Ellington, Irving Mills, Henry Nemo, and John Redmond   "I Let a Song Go Out of My Heart"

"I Let a Song Go Out of My Heart" by Duke Ellington, Irving Mills, Henry Nemo, and John Redmond. © 1938 (Renewed) by EMI Mills Music Inc., and Famous Music Corporation in USA. All Rights outside USA controlled by EMI Mills Music, Inc. All Rights Reserved. Used by permission of WARNER BROS. PUBLICATIONS U.S. INC., Miami, FL 33014 and Famous Music Corporation.

Duke Ellington and Mack David   "I'm Just a Lucky So-and-So"

10. **Very slow**

"I'm Just a Lucky So-and-So" by Duke Ellington and Mack David. Copyright © 1945 by Paramount Music Corp., Copyright renewed 1973. By permission of Duke Ellington Music c/o Famous Music.

E Ensembles

James Weldon Johnson and R. Rosamond Johnson   "Lift Every Voice And Sing" (National Negro Hymn)

Sing a song full of the hope that the pres - ent has brought us;
We have come, tread - ing our path thro' the blood of the slaugh - tered,
Lest our hearts, drunk with the wine of the world, we for - get Thee;

Fac - ing the ris - ing sun of our new day be - gun,
Out from the gloom - y past, till now we stand at last
Sha - dowed be - neath Thy hand, may we for - ev - er stand,

Let us march on till vic - to - ry is won.
Where the white gleam of our bright star is cast.
True to our God, true to our na - tive land.

5. Canon *a 2 cancrizans* (crabwise), retrograde   Bach *Musikalisches Opfer* (The Musical Offering), BWV 1079

6. Canon *a 2 cancrizans* (Kirnberger solution to #5):   top voice is no. 5 (left to right)
                                                          bottom voice is no. 5 (right to left)

Unit 14

A Rhythm—Simple Meter and Compound Meter: The Subtriplet

Section 1. Modules in Simple Meter

Begin by repeating each module several times. Then treat the successive modules as a continuous exercise.

Rhythm Syllables

Use the following syllables for the subtriplet if your instructor recommends you do so.

Section 2. Phrases in Simple Meter and Compound Meter with Subtriplets

6.

Section 3. Creating a Coherent Phrase in Simple Meter with Subtriplets

Return to section 1 and select three or four rhythm modules. Place the modules into a coherent four-measure phrase.

Write your solution on the following line:

B Diatonic, Chromatic, Whole-Tone, and Octatonic Models and Melodic Fragments for Interval Study

Section 1. Diatonic, Chromatic, Whole-Tone, and Octatonic Models

The models in this section emphasize modal mixture, enharmonic changes, motivic structure, chromatic, whole-tone, and octatonic fragments. The musical fragments (section 2) that correspond with each of the models in this section are as follows:

Models	Elements of Mixture		Fragments
1, 2	F♭		1
3, 4	F♭	D, C♭	2
5		C♭, B𝄫	3
6	F♭, E𝄫, D, C♭, B𝄫		4

Exercises 1–6

a. Mixture

The first four models contain elements of modal mixture. For practice, sing Example 1a, with one of your colleagues singing 1b, and so on.

b. Enharmonic changes (chromatic modulation)

Models	Enharmonic Changes	Fragments
7a, a', a"	A♭ = G♯	5
	G♭ = F♯	
	D♭ = C♯	
7b, 7b'		6

Exercise 7

The motives of examples 7a, 7a', and 7a" represent different orderings of the same intervallic patterns: M2, m3 (or M6), and P4. Examples 7b and 7b' represent the pattern: m2 and M3 (outlining a P4).

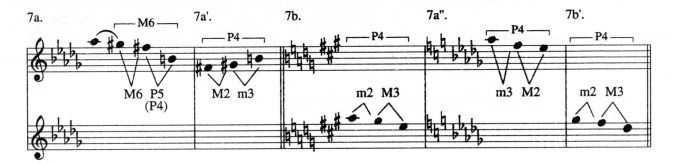

c. Motivic Structure

Models	Fragments
8a	7a, 7b
8b	8a, 8b

Exercise 8

d. Chromatic and whole-tone models

Models	Fragments
9a, b, c, d	9

Exercise 9

These models are extracted from a highly chromatic song by Liszt. Altogether, these three motives (9a, b, and c) outline a whole-tone scale. Motive 9d represents a whole-tone scale.

e. Octatonic models

Models	Fragments
10a, b, c, d	10

Exercise 10

These models are extracted from a melody line by Gershwin.

10a.   10b.   10c.   10d. Octatonic scale

t = 0   t = 3   t = 6

Section 2. Melodic Fragments—Intervals: All

(Note to the instructor: Relate the following melodic fragments to the models in part C.)

Sing the following melodic fragments until you can sing them without error.

a. Mixture

1.

Del Tredici   Alice Pleasance Liddell from *Final Alice* (transposed)

Andante sostenuto

Meas.   7   8   9   10   11   12

Meas.   21   22   23   24   25   26

2.

Liszt *Der Hirt* (The Shepherd) (transposed) (abridged)

Andante pastorale

Meas.   20   21   22   23

Meas.   83   84   88   89

Liszt *Pace non trovo* (I Find No Peace) (Petrarch Sonnet) (transposed)

3.

Agitato assai

4.

Prokofiev *Sladkaya pesenka* (Sweet Song), op. 68, no. 2

Andante

b. Modulation—enharmonic changes

5. Liszt *Der Fischerknabe (The Fisher Lad)*

DbM:

AM:

6. Liszt *Der Fischerknabe*

AM:

DbM:

c. Motivic structure

7a. Brahms Symphony no. 3, II (transposed)

7b. Brahms *Ballade,* op. 118, no. 3 (transposed)

8a. Brahms *Immer leiser wird mein Schlummer* (Fretful Slumber), op. 105, no. 2 (transposed)

8b. Brahms Piano Concerto no. 2, op. 83, III (transposed)

9. Liszt *Mignon Lied* (Mignon's Song) (transposed)

10. Gershwin "Promenade"

Section 3. Creating a Coherent Melody

Return to section 2 and select two or three segments of melodic fragments that would create a coherent melody. It may be necessary to change the meter and rhythm of certain segments, depending on your choice.

Section 4. Practice in Clef Reading: Alto, Tenor, and Soprano Clefs

Return to the melodic fragments of unit 10 for practice in clef reading. Substitute the alto clef for the treble clef and change the key signature. Return to the melodic fragments of unit 6 for practice in clef reading. Substitute the tenor clef for the treble clef and change the key signature. Return to the melodic fragments of unit 2 for practice in clef reading. Substitute the soprano clef for the treble clef and change the key signature.

C   Twentieth-Century Cabaret Songs by Kurt Weill, Benjamin Britten, and William Bolcom

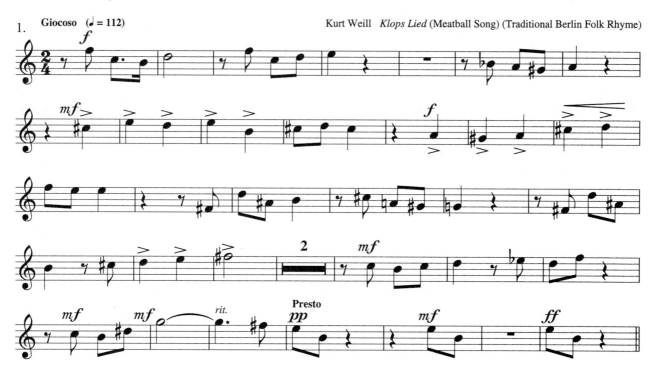

Benjamin Britten "Funeral Blues"

3.

William Bolcom "Waitin"

Simply ♩ = 60 or slower

D Twentieth Century Art Songs by Maurice Ravel, Gustav Holst, Hugo Weisgall, Elliott Carter, and Ellen Taaffe Zwilich

Ravel *Soupir* (Sigh), from *Trois Poèmes de Stéphane Mallarmé* (Three Poems of Stéphane Mallarmé), I (dedicated to Igor Stravinsky)

Ravel *Placet futile* (Futile petition), from *Trois Poèmes de Stéphane Mallarmé,* II (dedicated to Florent Schmitt)

Ravel *Surgi de la croupe et du bond* (Riding from the Crupper and the Leap), from *Trois Poèmes de Stéphane Mallarmé,* III
(dedicated to Erik Satie)

3.

Ravel *Kaddisch* (Kaddish) from *Deux Mélodies Hébraïques* (Two Hebrew Melodies)

4.

5. **Tranquillo** ♩ = 92

Ravel *L'Enigme Eternelle* (The Eternal Enigma) from *Deux Mélodies Hébraïques*

6. **Allegro**

Holst *Persephone*

Hugo Weisgall "The Cable Car" from *Lyrical Interval*

7. **Scorrevole; flowing eighths** (♩. = 108–112)

8.

Elliott Carter "The Rose Family"

Allegretto, con moto

"The Rose Family" by Elliot Carter. © 1947 (Renewed) by Associated Music Publishers, Inc. (BMI) Used by permission.

Ellen Taaffe Zwilich *Über die Felder* (Across the Fields), from *Einsame Nacht* (Lonesome Night)

9.   **Moderato (♪ = c. 104)**

"Across the Fields" ("Über die Felder") from *Einsamer Nacht (Lonesome Night)* by Ellen Taaffe Zwilich. © 1984 Merion Music, Inc. Used by permission of the publisher.

E Ensemble

Stravinsky *Perséphone*

Unit 15

A   Rhythm: Changing Meters

Section 1. Modules in Changing Meters

Consider each measure as a module to be practiced separately or as part of a continuous exercise. If the modules are treated as a continuous exercise, consider eighth notes as equivalent in simple meter, quarter as dotted quarter in compound, and so on.

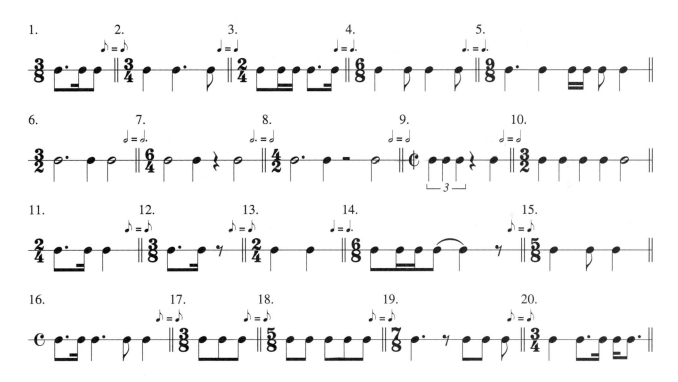

Section 2. Phrases in Changing Meters

1.

2.

9.

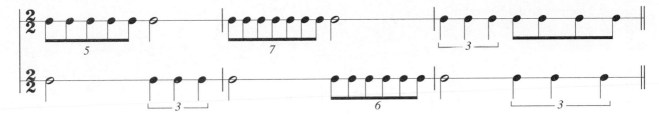

Section 3. Creating a Coherent Phrase in Changing Meters

Return to section 1 and select three or four rhythm modules. Place the modules into a coherent four-measure phrase.

Write your solution on the following line:

B Atonal Models and Melodic Fragments for Interval Study—Intervals: All

Section 1. Atonal Models

I. The exercises in this section are atonal.

Within the atonal context, a few whole-tone and octatonic patterns are found. All exercises relate to the music of Ives, Strauss, Schoenberg, Debussy, and Bartók and were composed between 1902 and 1921.

Each model in this section is related to the same corresponding number in the fragments. Each exercise has several segments (example 2: segments a–e) to encourage class participation by as many individuals as possible. One sings *a* while the next repeats *a* and continues with *b* and so on. For these atonal exercises, you should use whatever solfeggio or number system your instructor suggests.

Exercises 1 and 2

These two exercises emphasize the interval of the P4 in combination with M2s or m2s.

1a.   1b.   1c.

In exercise 2, the first two notes recur in patterns *a–e* and serve as an element of unity.

2a.   2b.   2c.   2d.   2e.

Exercises 3–5

Exercise 3 focuses on the M6 and m2.

Exercise 4 is a "Study in 7ths and Other Things," written in 1907 by Charles Ives.

Exercise 5 is also a "Study in 7ths."

Exercises 6 and 7

Exercise 6 is based on a six-note pattern (later known as pitch-class set 6–Z4).

Sing the outer voices; the inner voices are provided to establish context.

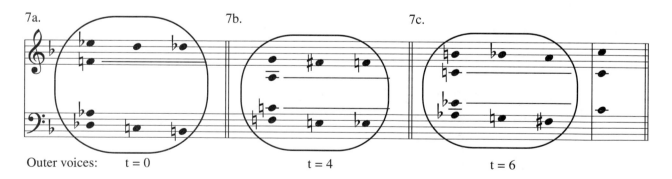

Exercises 8–13

Exercises 10–13 should be sung in ensemble.

Exercise 14

Exercise 14 is dedicated to all theory students who were inspired to write parallel fifths. Sing this in ensemble.

Section 2. Melodic Fragments—Intervals: All

Charles Ives "The Rainbow"

1.

2.

Charles Ives "From the Incantation" (abridged)

3.

R. Strauss *Salome*, op. 54

4.

Charles Ives "Soliloquy or a Study in Sevenths and Other Things" (abridged)

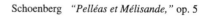

5.

Schoenberg *"Pelléas et Mélisande,"* op. 5

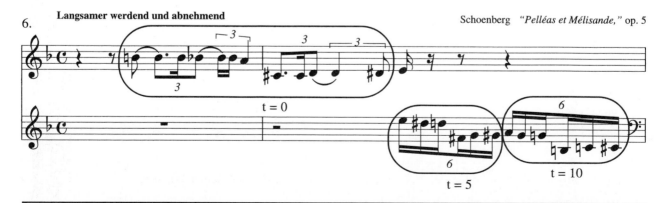

6.

Schoenberg *"Pelléas et Mélisande,"* op. 5

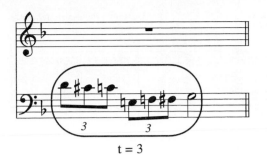

t = 3

Molto allegro

Strauss *Salome*

7.

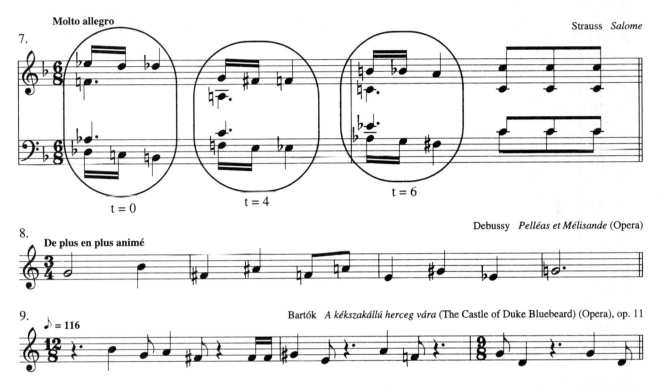

t = 0   t = 4   t = 6

8.

Debussy *Pelléas et Mélisande* (Opera)

De plus en plus animé

9.

Bartók *A kékszakállú herceg vára* (The Castle of Duke Bluebeard) (Opera), op. 11

♪ = 116

Strauss *Salome*

10.

Più mosso

11.

Schoenberg *Pelléas et Mélisande*, op. 5

In gehender Bewegung

12.

Bartók *The Castle of Duke Bluebeard*, op. 11

Meno mosso

13.

14. Fast and rough

Ives   "The New River"

© 1933 Merion Music, Inc. Used by permission of the publisher.

Section 3. Creating a Coherent Melody

Return to section 2 and select two or three segments of melodic fragments that would create a coherent melody. It may be necessary to change the meter and rhythm of certain segments, depending on your choice.

Section 4. Practice in Clef Reading: Alto, Tenor, and Soprano Clefs

Return to the melodic fragments of unit 11 for practice in clef reading. Substitute the alto clef for the treble clef and change the key signature. Return to the melodic fragments of unit 7 for practice in clef reading. Substitute the tenor clef for the treble clef and change the key signature. Return to the melodic fragments of unit 3 for practice in clef reading. Substitute the soprano clef for the treble clef and change the key signature.

C and D   Twentieth-Century Melodies for Careful Study and Preparation

This section contains works by Milhaud, Debussy, Menotti, Griffes, Bernstein, Weill, Trinkley, Barsom, and others.

Milhaud   *La Création du Monde* (The Creation of the World)

1.

Editions Max Eschig, Paris.

2.

Milhaud *La Création du Monde*

Flute

𝅗𝅥 = 54

Editions Max Eschig, Paris.

3.

Santa Rosalia by Bruce Trinkley, based on the painting by Fernando Botero. (libretto by Jason Charnesky)

Allegro agitato 𝅘𝅥 = 126

Oboe

4.

Paul Barsom "On Imminent Rays"

𝅘𝅥 = 60

con sord.

Cello

(slowly)

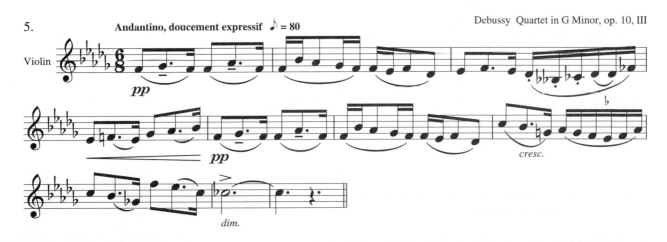

Copyright © 1989 Ringing Change Music. Reprinted by permission of Paul Barsom, State College, PA.

5.

Debussy Quartet in G Minor, op. 10, III

Andantino, doucement expressif 𝅘𝅥 = 80

Violin

6. **Triste et lente** (♩ = 44)

Debussy *Des pas sur la neige* (Footsteps in the Snow), Book I, Prelude VI

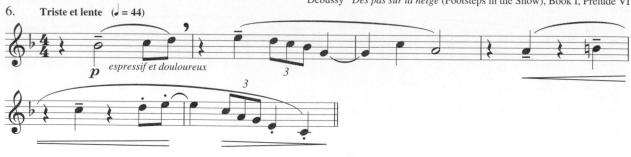

p *espressif et douloureux*

Debussy *La fille aux cheveux de lin* (The Girl with the Flaxen Hair), Book I, Prelude VIII

7.

p *sans rigeur*

8. **Allegretto, con moto**

Gian Carlo Menotti "The Black Swan" from *The Medium*

9. **Languidamente** (♩ = 72–80)

Charles T. Griffes Symphony in Yellow, op. 3, no. 2

10. **Very slowly and freely, like a folk song**

11.

Moderato assai

12.

Flute

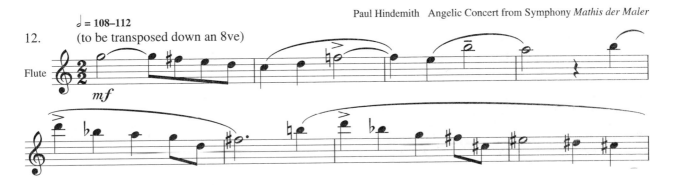

13.

♩ = 108–112

(to be transposed down an 8ve)

Hindemith   *Engelkonzert*, from *Symphonie Mathis der Maler*

Flute

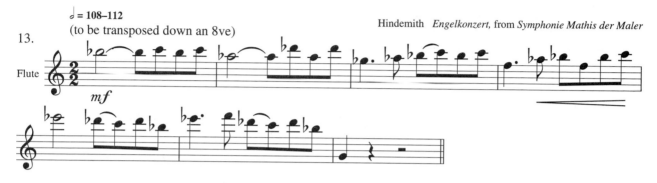

14.   **Allegro**   (♩. = 80)

Kodály   *Valsette*

15.

Béla Bartók   Bagatelle no. 1 from *Fourteen Bagatelles*, op. 6

Molto sostenuto   ♩ = 66

Presto ♩= 108
(to be transposed down an 8ve)

Béla Bartók   Bagatelle no. 14 from *Fourteen Bagatelles,* op. 6

16.

Munter. Schnelle Viertel
(to be transposed down an 8ve)

Hindemith   *Kleine Klaviermusik* (Short Piano Music), no. 3

17.

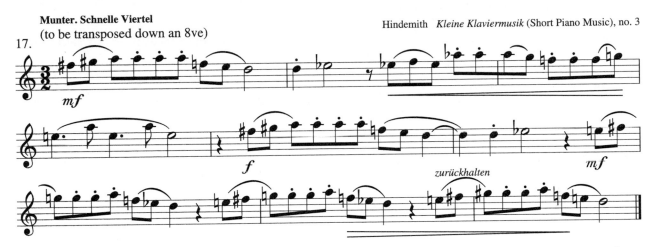

E   Ensembles of the Twentieth Century

The following ensemble excerpts should be performed vocally, although instruments may be used to supplement voices. In addition to singing or playing parts in ensemble, you are encouraged to play entire excerpts at the keyboard.

Procedure

1. Students should sing the melodic "reduction" of each excerpt, using whatever system is suggested by the instructor—solfege, numbers (1–8 or 0–11).
2. Students should take turns singing or playing individual lines of these excerpts before singing or playing them in ensemble.
3. Whenever possible, the instructor should bring recordings to class so that students will come to a full understanding of the musical context for each excerpt.

Examples 1 (Milhaud) and 2 (Hindemith) can be related to the melodic pattern, which encompasses six notes of the major scale:

1. from mi up to do (mi, fa, sol, la, ti, do), or
2. from 3 up to 1 (3, 4, 5, 6, 7, 1), or
3. from 4 up to 0 (4, 5, 7, 9, 11, 0)

1a.   Milhaud   *La Création du Monde*

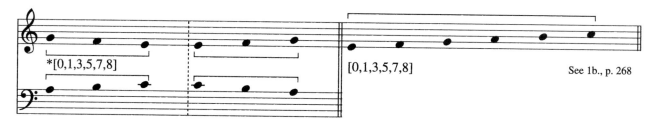

*[0,1,3,5,7,8]   [0,1,3,5,7,8]   See 1b., p. 268

Milhaud, "La Creation du Monde," (1923).

*For further explanation, see Allen Forte, *The Structure of Atonal Music.* New Haven, CT, Yale University Press, 1973.

2a.   Hindemith   *Engelkonzert,* from *Symphonie Mathis der Maler*

[0,1,3,5,7,8]   [0,1,3,5,7,8]

See 2b., p. 268

Example 3 (Debussy) introduces a recurring four-note pattern (tetrachord) in the second violin part, which encompasses four notes of the major scale:

1. from ti up to fa (ti, do, re, [mi], fa), or
2. from 7 up to 4 (7, 1, 2, [3], 4), or
3. from 11 up to 5 (11, 0, 2, [4], 5)

In the same example, the viola part has a recurring six-note pattern (hexachord), which can be thought of *at first* in two different tonalities:

1. first three notes: do, ti, sol; last three notes: re, fa, sol
2. first three notes: 1, 7, 5; last three notes: 2, 4, 5

Ultimately, students should be encouraged to think in terms of all twelve notes, with C being zero:

3. 7, 6, 2, 5, 8, 10

Whenever this six-note pattern is placed in "normal order" (see Forte's *Structure of Atonal Music*), the "pitch-class set" corresponds to 6Z39 in Forte's taxonomy.

2, 5, 6, 7, 8, 10 and reduced to "zero level" (Forte)
0, 3, 4, 5, 6, 8 and inverted
0, 2, 3, 4, 5, 8

3a.   Debussy   String Quartet, op. 10, II (m. 10)

See 3b., p. 271

Example 4 (Debussy) features a three-note pattern in various transformations (cello). Although it is possible to think of each three-note pattern in its own tonality (la, do, si; do, si, ti), it is more beneficial for the student to recognize the pattern of alternating M3s and m3s, or alternating "interval classes" (Forte), which form [0,1,4]:

ic 3 (interval class three), encompassing three half-steps = m3
ic 4 (interval class four), encompassing four half-steps = M3
In combination, the first six notes of the cello part are entirely chromatic.

In the same part (cello) at the end of the first measure, the last five notes are a d7 chord: 0,3,6,9. Both of these melodic ideas are prominent in measure 19:

Melodically, [0,1,4] is found in all four parts.
Harmonically, [0,3,6,9] is found when all four parts are combined.

4a.   Debussy String Quartet, op. 10, IV (m. 15)   meas. 19

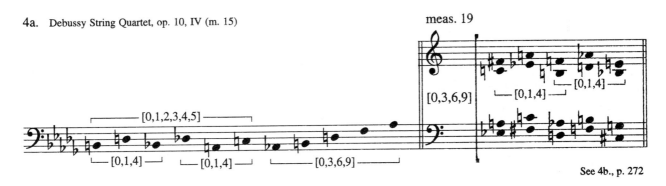

See 4b., p. 272

Example 5 (Hindemith) provides a wonderful opportunity for students to discover the sol, la, do, re pattern—sometimes referred to as the "I've Got Rhythm" tetrachord. The accompanimental parts are easily accessible for vocal or instrumental performance.

5a.   Hindemith   *Sing- und Spielmusiken* (Music to Sing and Play), from *Acht Kanons,* (Eight Canons), III, no. 2

See 5b., p. 273

1b. Clarinet parts are written in B♭

Milhaud *La Création du Monde*

Hindemith *Engelkonzert*, from *Symphonie Mathis der Maler*

2b.

3b.

Debussy String Quartet, op. 10, IV

15

En animant peu à peu ♩. = 108

5b.

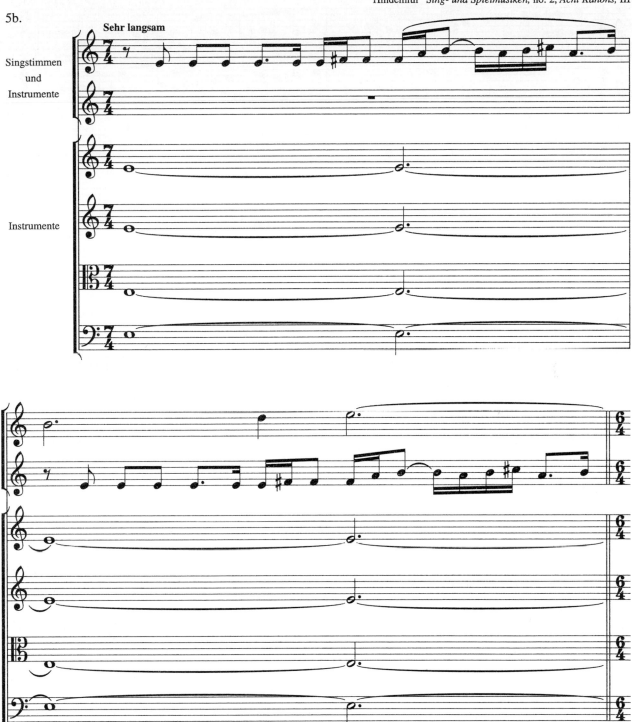

Unit 16

A Rhythm—Twentieth-Century Excerpt for Percussion

The entire class should participate in a reading of the opening bars of *Ionisation,* by Varèse.

Edgar Varèse *Ionisation*

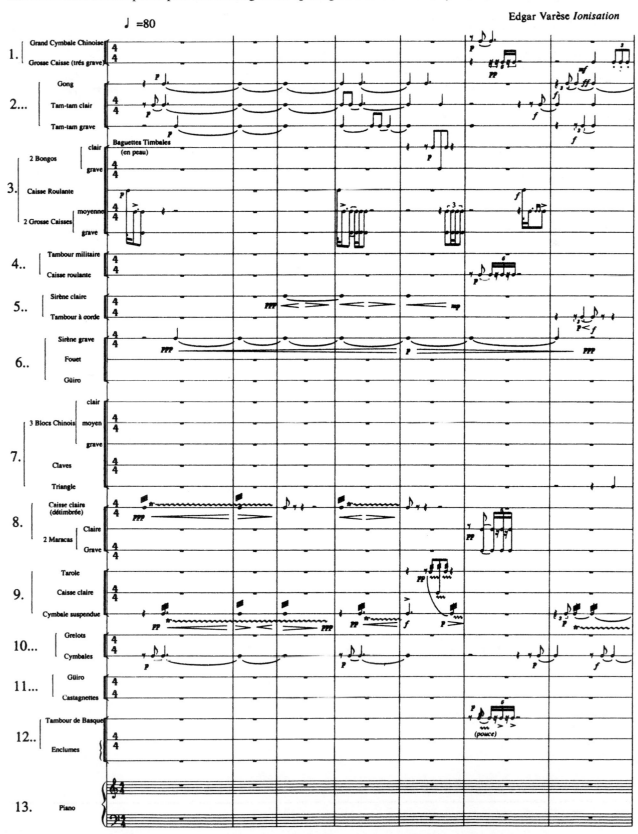

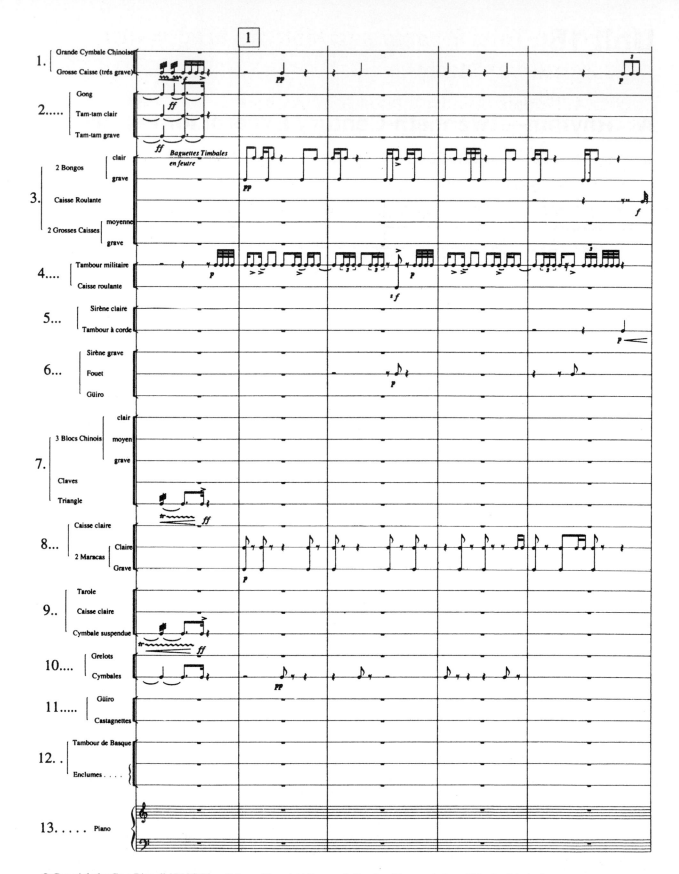

B Twelve-Tone Models and Melodic Fragments for Interval Study

Section 1. Models: Dyads, Trichords, Tetrachords, Pentachords, and Hexachords

All exercises in this section are of the twelve-tone type and relate to the first example (only) in section 2 (p. 278). The format for building exercises for interval study is illustrated for the first exercise. By using this approach, all twenty of the excerpts in section 2 will be made much easier to accomplish.

In order to provide as much individual participation as possible, the following procedure is recommended for in-class practice. Divide the row into two-note patterns (dyads)—the last note of each new dyad becomes the first note of the next dyad. One class member begins by singing *a* and another sings *b* and so on. The repeated note also facilitates the practice of tossing dyads.

a. Dyads

The drill can be expanded to include three-note (trichord), four-note (tetrachord), five-note (pentachord), and six-note (hexachord) patterns. This system will help you "ease" into the singing of twelve-tone melodies.

b. Trichords

c. Tetrachords

d. Pentachords

e. Hexachords

As you become more proficient, it should be possible to toss patterns at random. For some extra fun in class, one class member sings the first three notes and calls the name of another who, in turn, repeats the last pitch and the next three notes. You can continue this procedure through all ten melodies in section 2 (p. 278). In the following illustration, class members request the size of the pattern (i.e., dyad, trichord, etc.) as they are calling the student's name.

Section 2. Melodic Fragments: Twelve-Tone Sets

Each of the twenty melodies is a twelve-tone set, and all are excerpted from compositions by composers such as Schoenberg, Berg, and Webern. Most have been arranged to fit within a single voice range, and many have been rewritten in a rhythmic environment more suitable to vocal music.

Preparation for this assignment began earlier with the introduction of "Models for Interval Study" and "Melodic Fragments for Interval Singing."

Assuming that your expertise improved with the gradually increasing difficulty of the models and fragments in previous chapters, you should find these twelve-tone sets well within your mastery.

Section 3: Creating a Coherent Melody

Return to section 2 and select two or three segments of melodic fragments that would create a coherent melody. It may be necessary to change the meter and rhythm of certain segments, depending on your choice.

Section 4. Practice in Clef Reading: Alto, Tenor, and Soprano Clefs

Return to the melodic fragments of unit 12 for practice in clef reading. Substitute the alto clef for the treble clef and change the key signature. Return to the melodic fragments of unit 8 for practice in clef reading. Substitute the tenor clef for the treble clef and change the key signature. Return to the melodic fragments of unit 4 for practice in clef reading. Substitute the soprano clef for the treble clef and change the key signature.

C and D   Twentieth-Century Melodies for Careful Study and Preparation

Among the following melodies are works by Schoenberg, Berg, Webern, Stravinsky, Anderson, and Fenner.

Berg   Violin concerto, I A Carinthian Folk Tune

Berg   Violin Concerto, II, from *Es ist genug!* (It Is Enough), Bach chorale no. 216

3.

Schoenberg   *Verklärte Nacht* (Transfigured Night), op. 4

4.

Schoenberg   Chamber Symphony, op. 9

5.

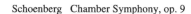

Webern   Passacaglia, op. 1

6.

7.

D. I. Music, P. O. Box 35, Lemont, PA 16851.

8.

T. J. Anderson "Street Song for Piano"

Copyright © 1980 Bote & Bock, a Boosey & Hawkes company. Reprinted by permission of Boosey & Hawkes, Inc.

9.

Stravinsky "Symphonies of Wind Instruments"

© Copyright 1926 by Hawkes & Son (London) Ltd. Copyright Renewed. Revised version © Copyright 1948, 1952 by Hawkes & Son (London) Ltd. Copyright Renewed. Reprinted by permission of Boosey & Hawkes, Inc.

10.

Berg *Wozzeck*

Copyright 1931 by Universal Edition A. G., Wien. Copyright Renewed. All Rights Reserved. Used by permission of European American Music Distributors Corporation, sole U.S. and Canadian agent for Universal Edition Vienna.

11.

12.

Stravinsky "In Memoriam Dylan Thomas"

Do not go gen-tle   in - to that good night,   Old age should burn and   rave at close of day;

Rage, rage a - gainst _ the dy   -   ing of the light . . . .

E Ensembles of the Twentieth Century

The following ensemble excerpts should be performed vocally, although instruments may be used to supplement voices. In addition to singing or playing parts in ensemble, you are encouraged to play entire excerpts at the keyboard.

Follow the same procedures as in unit 15E.

In example 1 (Fenner), the special charm of "The Sprightly Companion" is found in the symmetrical patterns of a nine-note scale: 0, 1, 2, 4, 5, 6, 8, 9, 10 in an imitative texture.

1a. Fenner "The Sprightly Companion" for Oboe and Tape III

See 1b., p. 287

Fenner "The Sprightly Companion" by Bruce Fenner. Reprinted by permission of D. I. Music, P.O. Box 35, Lemont, PA 16851.

In example 2 (Schoenberg), the twelve-tone row for the Quintet can be thought of as two hexachords: motives A and B.

2a. Schoenberg Quintet, op. 26, III

Used by permission of Belmont Music Publishers, Pacific Palisades, CA 90272.   See 2b., p. 288

In example 3 (Schoenberg), at least three significant tetrachords are audible in the "Introduction" to the Variations:

measures 4 and 7 [0,3,6,9]—"the diminished 7th tetrachord" also found in unit 15, example E-3, measure 19 of the Debussy Quartet

measure 6 [0,2,5,7]—"the sol, la, do, re" ("I've Got Rhythm") tetrachord, also found in unit 15, example E-5

measure 7 [0,3,4,7]—"the major-minor" tetrachord, or combinations of major and minor trichords

3a. Schoenberg Variations for Orchestra, op. 31

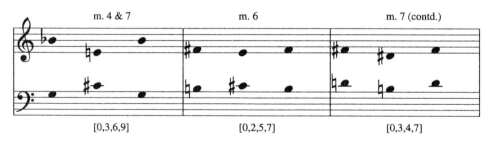

Used by permission of Belmont Music Publishers, Pacific Palisades, CA 90272.   See 3b., p. 288

In example 4 (Schoenberg), all twelve tones are found in measures 122 and 123. This twelve-tone piece can be used as a review of tetrachordal patterns.

Regarding example 5 (Anderson), in the composer's comment to Street Song, T. J. Anderson states: "Enculturation, the process of musically becoming, takes place for many people in children's game songs." This piece is based on a song that Mr. Anderson heard frequently while he was living in Atlanta, Georgia. The melody can be reduced to a six-note pattern:

E, D♯, E, C, A, G, C, D, C

In example 6, the atonal fugue (Berg) is based on a seven-note pattern. The vocal part, sung by Marie, depicts Mary Magdalene washing the feet of Jesus.

6a.   Berg   *Wozzeck*, op. 7 (1917–22)

[0,1,2,3,4,5,7]   [0,1,2,3,4,5,7]   See 6b., p. 290

Example 7 (Stravinsky) is taken from *Threni*, Stravinsky's first work to be written entirely in the twelve-tone serial technique. Notice that the excerpt gives two forms of the row: the original and the inversion.

7a.   Stravinsky   *Threni* (12-tone row)

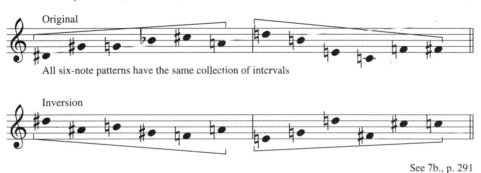

See 7b., p. 291

In example 8 (Stravinsky), the Carillon section of Stravinsky's *Firebird* (1910) has a wonderful atonal section, with multiple statements of a six-note pattern: [0,1,2,6,7,8] in the trumpet parts. As an experiment, students should transpose this pitch-class set at the tritone to see the order in which all six pitch classes will recur.

8a.   Stravinsky   *Firebird*, R-99 (transposed to concert pitch)

[0,1,2,6,7,8]   [0,1,2,6,7,8]   [0,1,2,6,7,8]

See 8b., p. 291

In example 9 (Stravinsky), the closing measures of *Firebird* (1910) consist of a series of major triads in first inversion, which "harmonize" two different forms of the *Firebird* motive: [0,1,2,6].

See 9b., p. 292

In example 10 (Webern), the third of Webern's five canons consists of four motives, which are labelled as A (4Z15), B (4–5), C (4–6), and D (4–4). The unity of this work is derived from the similarity among all of these motives, as indicated in the accompanying chart.

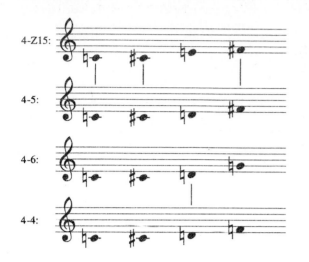

Webern *Five Canons*, op. 16, III

See 10b., p. 292

"The Sprightly Companion" by Bruce Fenner. Reprinted by permission of D. I. Music, P.O. Box 35, Lemont, PA 16851.

It will not be necessary to transpose these instrumental parts since they are written in concert pitch.

2b.

Schoenberg   *Bläserquintett* (Quintet for Wind Instruments), op. 26, III

Used by permission of Belmont Music Publishers, Pacific Palisades, CA 90272.

3b.

Schoenberg   *Variations for Orchestra,* op. 31

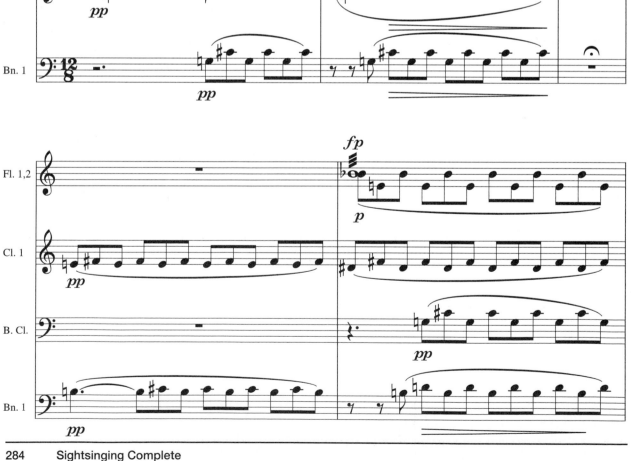

Etwas drängend

Schoenberg *String Trio,* op. 45

4b. **Very quiet** (♪ = 104)

8va

T. J. Anderson "Street Song for Piano"

5b. ♩ = ca. 88

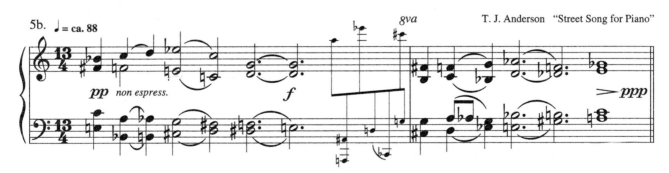

6b.

Grave (♩ = 56)

Berg *Wozzeck,* op. 7

Copyright 1931 by Universal Edition A. G., Wien. Copyright Renewed. All Rights Reserved. Used by permission of European American Music Distributors Corporation, sole U.S. and Canadian agent for Universal Edition A.G. Vienna.

7b.

In - ci - pit, in - ci - pit _____ la - men - ta - ti

In - ci - pit, la - men - ta - ti -

o Je - re - mi-ae Pro - phe - tae. _____

o Je - re - mi - ae Pro - phe - tae. _____

8b. **Allegro** (♩ = 120)   Stravinsky *L'oiseau de feu* (Firebird) (1910 Ballet)

Stravinsky *Firebird*

From *Firebird Ballet,* Melodies 8 & 9. Reprinted by permission of J. & W. Chester, Ltd., London.

Webern *Five Canons,* op. 16, III

10b.

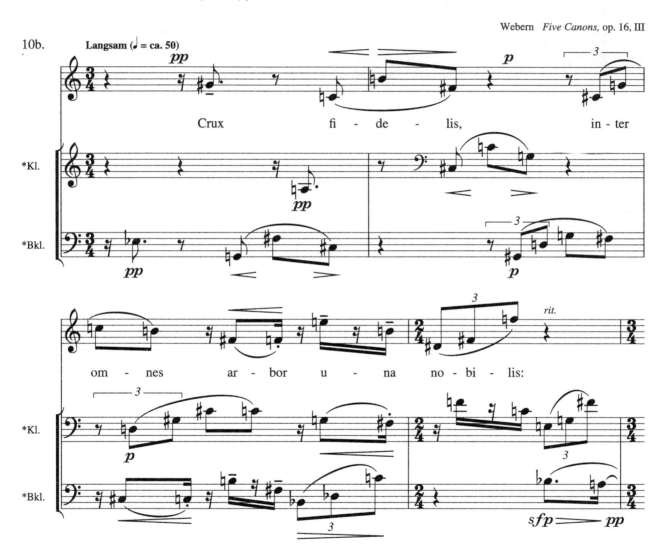

nul - la   sil - va   ta - lem pro - fert,

*Kl.

*Bkl.

* Clarinets sound at concert pitch

Composer and Genre Index

A

Amish hymnody. "Author of the Whole Creation," 24; "Come Ye Sinners," 23; "Great Physician, The," 24; "Jesus, Jesus, Source of Life," 23; "Jesus, Lover of My Soul," 23; "Praise God Forever," 24; "Thousand Times by Me Be Greeted," 24; "When the Due Time Had Taken Place," 24.

Anderson, T. J. *Street Song* for Piano, 278, 285.

B

Bach, Johann Sebastian. (BWV 768), var. 10, "Sei ge grüsset, Jesu gütig," 186; *Brandenburg Concerto* no. 2, I, 90; Cantata no. 4, 120; Cantata no. 5, 120; Cantata no. 42, 120; Cantata no. 46, 120; Cantata no. 72, 120; Cantata no. 75, 120; Cantata no. 89, 120; Cantata no. 144, 121; Cantata no. 189, 121; Cantata no. 197, 121; Chorale 48, *Ach wie nichtig, ach wie flüchtig*, 18; Chorale 78, 132; Chorale 91, *Verlieh' uns Frieden gnädiglich*, 54; Chorale 126, 132; Chorale 134, 132; Chorale 152, *Meinem Jesum laß' ich nicht, weil*, 54; Chorale 161, *Ihr Gestirn', ihr hohlen Lüfte*, 54; Chorale 163, *Für Freuden laßt uns springen*, 54; Chorale 164, *Herr Gott, dich loben alle wir*, 54; Chorale 170, 132; Chorale 172, 133; Chorale 178, 133; Chorale 198, *Christus, der uns selig macht*, 54; Chorale 245, *Christe, der du bist Tag und Licht*, 54; Chorale 246, *Singt dem Herrn ein neues Lied*, 54; *English Suite* no. 3, Gavotte II, 90; *English Suite* no. 5, Gigue, 117; *French Suite* no. 3, Sarabande, 117; *French Suite* no. 6, Allemande, 116; *In dulci jubilo* (BWV 608), canon, 109; *Klavierbüchlein für W. F. Bach* (BWV 841), Menuet 1, 123; *Kunst der Fuge, Die* (Art of the Fugue), no. 5, 124; no. 9, 117; no. 12, rectus, 39; inversus, 39; no. 13, rectus, 123; inversus, 123; Overture in F Major (BWV 820), Bourée, 123; Gigue, 123; Trio, 123; *Muikalisches Opfer* (BWV 1079), 174, 231; *Partita* no. 2, Rondeau, 116; *Partita* no. 6, Gavotte, 116; *Three-Part Inventions*, no. 2, 174; *Two-Part Inventions*, no. 2, 175; no. 4, 174; *Well-Tempered Clavier* I, Fugue 4, 217; Fugue 10, 117; Fugue 24, 176.

Barber, Samuel. *Bessie Bobtail* (op. 2, no. 3), 91; *I Hear an Army*, 157; *Mélodies passagères* (op.

Barber, Samuel—Cont.
27), no. 4, "Le clocher chante," 179; *Rain Has Fallen*, 159; *Vanessa*, "Under the Willow Tree," 91.

Barsom, Paul. *On Imminent Rays*, 257.

Bartók, Béla. *A kékszakállú herceg vára* (op. 11), 255; *Bagatelles* (op. 6), no. 1, 260; no. 14, 261; *Mikrokosmos* II, "Méditation," 95.

Basie, Count. *See also* Rushing, James, Count Basie, and Ed Durham. *King Joe (Joe Louis Blues)*, 222.

Basie, Count, Jerry Livingston, and Mack David. *Blue and Sentimental*, 223.

Beethoven, Ludwig van. *Das Gluck der freundschaft* (op. 88), 104; *Der Mann von Wort* (op. 99), 104; *Fidelio* (op. 72c), overture, 84; *Freundschaft* (WoO 164), 166; *Missa Solemnis* (op. 123), Benedictus, 25; Credo, 25; Gloria, 25; (op. 52), no. 1, "Urians Reise um die Welt," 104; no. 2, "Feuerfarb'," 104; Piano Concerto no. 5 (op. 73), II, 102; Sonata (op. 10, no. 1), I, 102; Sonata (op. 10, no. 3), I, 116; Sonata (op. 111), I, 218; Sonata for Violoncello and Piano (op. 69), I, 95; String Quartet (op. 18, no. 3), 102; String Quartet (op. 18, no. 4), 102; String Quartet (op. 130), IV, 132; String Quartet (op. 131), IV, 131; VII, 132; String Quartet (op. 132), I, 174; String Quartet (op. 133, Grosse Fuge), I, 174, 175; String Quartet (op. 135), III, 132; Symphony no. 1 (op. 21), I, 133; Symphony no. 2 (op. 36), III (Trio), 20; Symphony no. 5 (op. 67), II, 195; IV, 21; Symphony no. 6 (op. 68), III, 20; Symphony no. 7 (op. 92), II, 21; III, 21; IV, 21; Symphony no. 8 (op. 93), I, 21; Symphony no. 9 (op. 125), IV (Freude), 22; Three Sonatas (WoO 47), no. 3, II, var. 2, 103; var. 6, 103; Two Sonatinas, 103. *Variations on "God Save the King,"* (WoO 78), 196; (WoO 50), II, 124; (WoO 80), theme, 194; (WoO 191), 125; (WoO 192), 125; (WoO 193), 125.

Belafonte, Harry, and Lord Burgess. *Island in the Sun*, 224.

Berg, Alban. Violin Concerto, I, 158; Carinthian folk melody, 276; II, 277; Bach Chorale, *Es ist genug!*, 216, 276; *Wozzeck* (op. 7), 278, 280, 286.

Berlioz, Hector. *Te Deum*, "Dignare Domine," 182.

Bernstein, Leonard. *Candide*, "It Must Be Me," 259.

Bolcom, William. *Waitin'*, 241.

Bradford, Perry. *Crazy Blues*, 221; *That Thing Called Love*, 220–21.

Brahms, Johannes. (op. 6), no. 1, "Spanisches Lied," 185; (op. 7), no. 3, "Anklänge," 184; (op. 69), no. 5, "Tambourliedchen," 184; (op. 71), no. 2, "An den Mond," 185; (op. 84), no. 5, "Spannung," 184; (op. 86), no. 1, "Therese," 184; no. 4, "Uber die Heide," 185; (op. 95), no. 4, "Der Jäger," 185; (op. 97), no. 6, "Trennung," 185; (op. 105), no. 2, "Immer leiser wird mein Schlummer," 239; *Ballade* (op. 118), no. 3, 239; Piano Concerto no. 2 (op. 83), III, 239; *Romanzen aus Magelone* (op. 33), no. 5, "So willst du des Armen dich gnädig erbarmen?" 185; Symphony no. 3, II, 239; *Thirteen Canons* (op. 113), no. 11, "Ich weiss," 210.
Britten, Benjamin. *Funeral Blues*, 241.
Bruckner, Anton. Symphony no. 5, II, 124.

C

Cadman, Charles Wakefield. *He Who Moves in the Dew*, 203.
Calloway, Cab. *See* Perkins, Frank.
Calypso. "Back Down to the Tropics," 47; "Land of the Humming Bird," 36; "Mattie Rag," 47; "Ratta Madan Law," 47.
Carter, Elliott. *The Rose Family*, 247.
Casséus, Frantz. *Nan fond bois*, 67.
Chopin, Frédéric. Etude (op. 10, no. 9), 62; Nocturne (op. 9, no. 2), 62; Nocturne (op. 15, no. 3), 62; Nocturne (op. 27, no. 2), 62; Nocturne (op. 55, no. 2), 62; Nocturne (op. 62, no. 2), 62.
Couperin, François. *Les Moissonneurs*, 108.

D

David, Mack. *See* Basie, Count, with Jerry Livingston, and Mack David; Ellington, Duke, with Mack David.
Debussy, Claude. *Pelléas et Mélisande*, 255, 256; *Préludes* Book I, no. 6, "De pas sur la neige," 258; no. 8, "La fille aux cheveux de lin," 258; String Quartet in G Major (op. 10), II, 267; III, 257; IV, 268; *Three Ballades of François Villon*, no. 3, "Des femmes de Paris," 158.
Del Tredici, David. *Final Alice*, "Alice Pleasance Liddell," 238.
Durham, Ed. *See* Rushing, James, Count Basie, and Ed Durham.

E

Ebb, F., and J. Kander. *New York, New York* theme, 224.
Ellington, Duke. Sacred Concert no. 1, "Come Sunday," 182; "David Danced," 181; (with Mack David) *I'm Just a Lucky So-and-So*, 228; (with Harry James and Don George) *Everything but You*, 227; (with Irving Mills and Albany Bigard) *Mood Indigo*, 216, 226; (with Irving Mills and Manny Kurtz) *In a Sentimental Mood*, 226; (with Irving Mills, Henry Nemo, and John Redmond) *I Let a Song Go Out of My Heart*, 228; (with Irving Mills and Rex Stewart) *Boy Meets Horn*, 225; (with Eddie DeLange and Irving Mills) *Solitude*, 225; (with Billy Strayhorn) *Day Dream*, 226; (with Paul Webster) *I Got It Bad*, 227.
Ezrachi, Y. *Yesh Banu Ko-ach*, 200.

F

Fenner, Burt. *The Sprightly Companion* for Oboe and Tape, III, 280, 283.
Folk song. *See also* Calypso, Irish folk songs, Jewish songs. *Africa.* "Chant des chrétiens d'ethiopie," 178; "Dubula," 84; "Ronde des enfant au claire de lune," 92–95; *America.* "Driving Saw-Logs on the Plover," 121; "How We Got Up to the Woods Last Year," 86; "I Am a River Driver," 86; "Raftsmen's Song, The," 86; "Save Your Money While You're Young," 122. *Appalachia.* "Barbara Ellen," 198. *Bulgaria.* Folk song, 202. *Creole* (Louisiana). "Aine, dé, trois, Caroline," 65; "Aurore Pradère," 63; "Belle Layotte," 64; "Dialogue d'Amour," 65; "Gardé piti mulet là," 64; "Quand mo-té jeune," 64. *Florida.* "King and Queen," 34. *French-Canadian.* "La Bastringue," 34. *Greece.* Folk song in Dorian mode, 198. *Haiti.* "Quitta Mouille," 99; untitled songs (four), 122–23. *Jamaica.* "Cookie," 69; "Cudelia Brown," 70; folk song, 55, rhythmic framework, 43; "Mattie walla lef," 62; "Mattie Rag," 62; "Wata come a me eye," 69; *Madagascar.* "Mon coeur est en peine," 70–75. *Russia.* "My Sweetheart," 201. *Santería.* Ochún (rhythmic structure), 80, 82. *Spain.* "Navalafuente," 203. *Switzerland.* "Voici la mi-ete," 87; "Z' Basel an Mym Rhy," 86; *Tahiti.* "Adieux a Taïti," 87.
Franck, César. Violin Sonata, II, 158.

G

Gershwin, George. *Promenade*, 239.

Gregorian Chant. Dies Irae—Requiem Mass, 197; Veni Sancte Spiritus (Come Holy Spirit)—Pentecost (abridged), 5; Hymn to St. Thomas Aquinas, 182; In Paradisum, 182; Jesu dulcis memoria, 182; Kyrie IX (*Cum jubilo*), 38; Kyrie XI (*Orbis factor*), 38; Kyrie eleison (Lord Have Mercy)—Requiem Mass, 5; Sanctus IX (*Cum jubilo*), 38.

Griffes, Charles Tomlinson. (op. 3), no. 2, "Symphony in Yellow," 258.

H

Handel, George Frederic. *Julius Caesar*, act 1, 119; Suite no. 1 (HWV.434), Minuet, 106; Suite no. 3 (HWV.428), Var. 4, 107; Suite no. 4 (HWV.437), Var. 1, 107; Suite no. 5 (HWV.430), Air ("The Harmonious Blacksmith"), 107; Suite no. 7 (HWV.440), Gigue, 106; Suite no. 8 (HWV.441), Gigue, 107; Suite no. 9 (HWV.442), Chaconne, 106; Var. 62, 108; *Wassermusik*, 4 Suite no. 1 (HWV.348), 106; 8 Suite no. 1 (HWV.348), 106; 12 Suite no. 2 (HWV.349), 106.

Haydn, Franz Joseph. Allegro molto in D Major (fragment), 22; Canon, 109; Capriccio (Hob. XVII:1), 22; *Dir nah ich mich, nah mich dem Throne*, 176; Hob. XVI:3, 22; Hob. XVI:12, III, 22; Minuet in G Major (Hob. XVI:11), III, 23; Nine Early Sonatas, no. 9, III, 23; Sonata (Hob. XVI:5), 217; Sonata (Hob. XVI:12), 175; Sonata (Hob. XVI:16), 175; Sonata in D Major (Hob. XVI:51), II, 22; String Quartet (op. 74, no. 3), I, 218; String Quartet (op. 76, no. 4), I, 216, 217; *strickende Mädchen, Das*, 216, 217; Symphony no. 88, II, 101; Symphony no. 94, II, 32, 101; III, 32; Variations (Hob. XVII:2), var. 2, 22; var. 16, 22; Variations (Hob. XVII:5) theme, 22.

Hensel, Fanny Mendelssohn. *Schwanenlied*, 210.

Hindemith, Paul. *Kleine Klaviermusik*, no. 3, 261; *Sing- und Speilmusiken*, no. 2, 269–70; *Symphonie Mathis der Maler*, "Engelkonzert," 259, 260, 264–66.

Holst, Gustav. *Persephone*, 245–46.

I

Irish folk songs. "Bold Child, A," 198; "Blackthorn Tree, The," 203; "Christmas Carol or Hymn from Mrs. Close," 193; "Coulin, The" (lament), 6; "Da Luain, da Mairt," 66; "Derreen Day," 178; Dies Irae as sung in Co. of Londonderry, 197; "Eliza," 198; "Fair Hills of E'ire, O! The," 202; "Farewell to Carraig An Éide," 181; "Funeral Cry, Galway, August 28th, 1840," 183; "Hymn Sung on the Dedication of a Chapel, Co. of Londonderry," 183; "I Will Walk with My Love," 68; "Lillibulero," 69; "Lone Rock, The," 201; "New Song Called Granuaile, A," 68; "Piper's Tunes, The," 68; "Precious Treasure, The," 178; "Soft Deal Board, The," 202; "'Tis the Last Rose of Summer," 181; "Young Lad," 201.

Ives, Charles. *From the Incantation*, 254; *New River, The*, 256; *Soliloquy, or a Study in Sevenths and Other Things*, 252.

J

Jewish songs. *See also* Songs of the Babylonian Jews. "Adon Olam," 47; "Artsah Alinu," 200; "Ets Chayim Hi," 49; "Hasivenu Elecha," 50; "Hevenu Shalom Aleychem," 47; "Hin'ni Muchan Um'zuman," 48; "L'cha Dodi," 48; "Praise to the Living God—Yigdal," 48; "Sim Shalom," 49; "Yismach Mosche," 48.

Johnson, James Weldon, and Rosamund Johnson. *Lift Every Voice and Sing*, 229–30.

Josquin des Près. *See* Près, Josquin des.

K

Kodály, Zoltán. *Valsette*, 260.

L

Lassus, Orlande de. Benedictus, 26.

Leach, Tony. *He's Worthy to Be Praised*, 76–78.

Liszt, Franz. *Fischerknabe, Der*, 239; *Freudvoll und leidvoll*, 216, 217; *Hirt, Der*, 238; *Mignon Lied*, 239; *Pace non trovo*, 238; *Vätergruft, Die*, 218.

Livingston, Jerry. *See* Basie, Count, with Jerry Livingston, and Mack David.

M

Mahler, Alma. *Erkennende, Der*, 209.

Mahler, Gustav. *Kinder-Totenlieder*, "Nun will die Sonn' so hell aufgehn!" 208; *Knaben Wunderhorn, Des*, "Wer hat dies liedlein erdacht?" 85; *Lied von der Erde, Das*, "Trinklied vom Jammer der Erde, Das," 207; "Abschied, Der," 187; "Einsame im Herbst, Der," 207; "Von der Jugend," 208; *Lieder eines fahrenden Gesellen*, no. 1, "Wenn mein Schatz Hochzeit," 209; no. 2, "Ging heut' Morgen über's Feld," 209; *Tambourgs'sell, Der*, 208.

Martinu, Bohuslav. *Kvet Broskví*, 179.

McFarlane, Kathleen. *The Laughter of Raindrops*, 66; [untitled], 67.

Mendelssohn, Felix. *Songs Without Words* (op. 30), no. 3, "Consolation," 163; no. 6, "Venetian Gondola Song," 163; *Songs Without Words* (op. 53), no. 2, "The Fleecy Cloud," 164; no. 4, "Sadness of Soul," 164; *Songs Without Words* (op. 62), no. 1, "May Breezes," 164; no. 6, "Spring Song," 164; *Songs Without Words* (op. 85), no. 4, "Elegy," 164; *Songs Without Words* (op. 102), no. 2, "Retrospection," 165; no. 3, "Tarantella," 165; no. 6, "Belief," 165.

Menotti, Giancarlo. *The Medium*, "The Black Swan," 258.

Milhaud, Darius. *La Création du Monde*, 256, 257, 264.

Mills, Irving. *See* Ellington, Duke, with Irving Mills and Albany Bigard; Ellington, Duke, with Irving Mills and Manny Kurtz; Ellington, Duke, with Irving Mills, Henry Nemo, and John Redmond; Ellington, Duke, with Irving Mills and Rex Stewart.

Mozart, Wolfgang Amadeus. *Abendempfindung* (K.523), 138; *An Chloe* (K.524), 137; *Clemenza di Tito, La*, 194, 195; *Cosí fan tutte* (K.588), no. 10, Terzettino, 150–51; *Dans un bois solitaire* (K.308/295b), 134; Eight Minuets (K.315g), 32; *Entführung aus dem Serail, Die*, 196; *finta giardiniera, La*, 194, 196; German Dance no. 5 (K.509), 18, 85; *Gesellenreise (Freimaurerlied)* (K.468), 134, 136; Horn Concerto (K.417), III, 132; Horn Concerto (K.447), I, 101; II, 101; III, 101; Horn Concerto (K.495), I, 131; II, 101; *Idomeneo*, Act I, Aria (Elektra), 45, 46; *Im Frühlingsanfang* (K.597), 137; *Kinderspiel, Das* (K.598), 135; *kleine Nachtmusik, Eine* (A Little Night Music) (K.525), I, 45, 101; *kleinen Friedrichs Geburtstag, Des* (K.529), 135; Minuet no. 2 (K.2), 84; *noces de Figaro, Les*, 194, 195; *O Heiliges Band* (K.148/125h), 134; *Requiem* (K.626), Lacrymosa, 84; Sanctus, 18; Tuba mirum, 84; *Selig, selig, selig, alle* (K.230), 141, 142, 143; *Sehnsucht nach dem Frühlinge* (K.596), 137;

Mozart, Wolfgang Amadeus—Cont.
Sie, sie ist dahin (K.229), 144, 145–48; String Quartet (K.458), I, 96; *Traurig, doch gelassen* (K.391/340b), 134; *Un moto di Gioja* (K.579), 134, 138; Variations on a Minuet by Duparc (K.573), theme, 32; *Verschweigung, Die* (K.518), 135, 138; *Warnung* (K.433/416c), 136; *Zufriedenheit, Die* (K.349/367a), 134; *Zufriedenheit, Die* (K.473), 136; *Zufriedenheit im Niedrigen Stande, Die* (K.151/125f), 134; *Zum Schluss* (K.484), 135.

Musorgsky, Modest. *Boris Godunov*, Polonaise, 201; act 1, scene 1, 158; scene 2, 84.

N

Negro Spiritual. *Deep River*, 182.

P

Pergolesi, Giovanni B. *Adriano in Syria*, "Contento forse vivere nel mio martir potrei," 140; *La serva padrona*, act 1, 120.

Perkins, Frank and Cab Calloway. *The Skat Song*, 222.

Près, Josquin des. *Missa de Beata Virgine*, Kyrie, 39.

Primrose, Joe. *St. James Infirmary*, 66.

Prokofiev, Serge. (op. 68), no. 4, "Sladkaya pesenka," 238; (op. 104), no. 4, "Katerina," 202–3.

Puccini, Giacomo. *Gianni Schicchi*, 119.

Purcell, Henry. *King Arthur*, Frost scene, 196.

R

Rameau, Jean-Philippe. *Les Indes galantes*, 139.

Ravel, Maurice. *Deux Mélodies Hébraïques*, "L'Enigme Eternelle," 245; "Kaddish," 244; *Trois poems de Stéphane Mallarmé*, "Placet futile," 242–43; "Soupir," 242; "Surgi de la croupe et du bond," 243.

Rossini, Gioachino. *William Tell*, overture, 90.

Rushing, James, Count Basie, and Ed Durham. *Good Morning Blues*, 223.

S

Schoenberg, Arnold. Chamber Symphony (op. 9), 277; *Pelléas et Mélisande* (op. 5), 254, 255; Quintet for Winds (op. 26), III, 280, 284; String Trio (op. 45), 285; Variations for Orchestra (op. 31), 280, 284–85; *Verklärte Nacht* (op. 4), 277.

Schubert, Franz. *Am Flusse* (D. 766), 51; *Am Meer*, 217; *Atlas, Der*, 217; *Doppelgänger, Der*, 217; *Drang in die Ferne* (D.770), 52; *Ecossaise* (D.421), 90; Fantasy for Piano and Violin (op. 159), 186; *Ihr Bild*, 159; *Musensohn, Der* (D.764a), 52; *schöne Mullerin, Die* (D.795), no. 17, "Die böse Farbe," 207; *Schwanengesang* (D.318), no. 5, "Aufenhalt," 51; *Schweizerlied* (D.559), 51; Symphony no. 5, Minuet, 45, 46; Symphony no. 8 ("Unfinished") (D.759), I, 53; *Winterreise* (op. 89, D.911), no. 4, "Estarrung," 51; no. 5, "Der Lindenbaum," 52; no. 6, "Wasserflut," 204; no. 8, "Rückblick," 204; no. 10, "Rast," 204; no. 12, "Einsamkeit," 205; no. 13, "Die Post," 205; no. 17, "Im Dorfe," 206; no. 18, "Der Stürmische," 206; no. 19, "Täuschung," 206; no. 21, "Das Wirtshaus," 206; no. 24, "Der Leiermann," 52; Variation on a Waltz by Diabelli (D.718), 85; *Zwei Szenen aus "Lacrimas"* (op. 124, no. 1, D.857 [2]), II (Delphine), 52.

Schumann, Clara. (op. 13), no. 5, "Ich hab' in deinem Auge," 161; (op. 23), no. 1, "Was weinst du, Blümlein," 161; Piano Trio, 161; *Three Songs* (Rückert) (op. 12), "Er ist gekommen in Sturm und Regen," 160; "Leibst du um Schönheit," 160; "Warum willst de andre fragen?" 160.

Schumann, Robert. (op. 25), no. 1, "Widmung," 161; (op. 27), no. 3, "Was soll ich sagen," 162; (op. 30), no. 3, "Der Hidalgo," 162; (op. 35), no. 2, "Stirb, Lieb' und Freud!" 162; no. 10, "Stille Thränen," 163; (op. 36), no. 3, "Nichtes Schöneres," 163; *Albumblätter* no. 5 (op. 99), no. 8, 89; no. 13, Scherzo, 89; *Album for the Young* (op. 68), no. 3, "Trällerliedchen," 87; no. 5, "Stücken," 88; no. 8, "Wilder Reiter," 88; no. 18, "Schnitterliedchen," 89; no. 19, "Kleine Romanze," 89; no. 24, "Ernteliedchen," 89; *Papillons* (op. 2), no. 3, 88; no. 12, "Finale," 88.

Schütz, Heinrich. *sieben Worte Jesu Christi, Die*, Introitus, 211–12.

Sinatra, Frank. *See* Ebb, F. and J. Kanden.

Smith, Chris. *Ballin' the Jack*, 219; *Boom, Tum, Ta-Ra-Ra—Zing Boom!*, 219.

Songs of the Babylonian Jews. Idelsohn Collection. *im afês—Selihot* (Forgivness), 5; *hôdu* (Praise)—Passover, 5.

Strauss, Richard. *Salome* (op. 54), 254, 255.

Stravinsky, Igor. *Berceuse*, 199; *Firebird*, 281, 287, 288; *Histoire pour enfants*, no. 1, "Timlimbom," 177; *In Memoriam Dylan Thomas*, 279; *Perséphone*, 248; *Petrushka*, 116; 3rd tableau, 158; *Quatre chants russe*, no. 1, "Canarde," 180; no. 2, "Chanson pour compter," 180; *sacre du printemps, Le*, 279; *Symphonies of Wind Instruments*, 278; *Threni*, 281, 287.

Strayhorn, Billy, and the Delta Rhythm Boys. *See also* Ellington, Duke, with Billy Strayhorn. *Take the 'A' Train*, 225.

T

Tchaikovsky, Pyotr. Symphony no. 5 (op. 64), I, 85.
Telemann, Georg Philipp. Fuga 2, 166–67.
Trinkley, Bruce. *Santa Rosalia*, 257.

V

Varèse, Edgar. *Ionisation*, 271–72.
Verdi, Guiseppe. *Aïda*, act 3, Aïda and Amonasro duet, 118; Aïda and Radames duet, 119; act 4, 116; *Attila*, act 2, 119; *Nabucco*, "Chorus of the Hebrew Slaves," 118; "Chorus of the Levites," 118; "Mio furor, non più costretto," 118.

W

Wagner, Richard. *fliegende Holländer, Die*, overture, 45, 46; *Götterdämmerung*, Prelude, 176; act 3, 157; scene 1, 116, 176; scene 2, 116, 176; scene 3, 116, 158.
Webern, Anton. Passacaglia (op. 1), 281; Five Canons (op. 16), III, 282, 288.
Weill, Kurt. *Klops Lied*, 240; *Lonesome Dove, The*, 259.
Weisgall, Hugo. *Lyrical Interval*, "The Cable Car," 246.

Z

Zwillich, Ellen Taaffe. *Einsame Nacht*, "Uber die Felder," 247.